OFF BOOK

OFF
BOOK

MEMORIZATION SECRETS
FROM PERFORMING ARTISTS

BRENT SVERDLOFF

Epigraph Books
Rhinebeck, New York

Off Book: Memorization Secrets from Performing Artists
Copyright © 2022 by Brent Sverdloff

Paperback ISBN: 978-1-954744-65-3
eBook ISBN: 978-1-954744-66-0

Library of Congress Control Number: 2022904082

Book and cover design by Colin Rolfe
Cover painting: "Maquettes de Théatre 15" (1930) by Alexandra Exter

Epigraph Books
22 East Market Street, Suite 304
Rhinebeck, NY 12572
(845) 876-4861
epigraphps.com

"Your imagination must become as real and important to you as your memories and feelings."
—HAROLD GUSKIN, *How to Stop Acting*

CONTENTS

Performing One's Own Work

Monologues

Muscle Memory and Repetition

Special Techniques

The Playwright's Perspective

Blanking and Getting Back on Track ————————————

Playing Together ————————————

Foreign and Technical Language ————————————

Doubling Up ————————————

Stage vs. Television ————————————

INTRODUCTION

B ack in August 2015, I went to see comedian Colin Quinn perform *The New York Story,* his salty valentine to his hometown. Nearly 200 of us were packed into the intimate Cherry Lane Theater, excited at being so close to a comic at the top of his game. Quinn rambled around the stage, a cluttered set meant to evoke the row houses of his bygone Brooklyn neighborhood. With his trademark restless energy, he spun yarn after yarn about the many ethnic groups that have shaped the city. Quinn was an equal opportunity offender; no group escaped his hilarious barbs, which were loaded with vivid details and relied on precise sequencing and timing.

Like most people, I marvel at how stage actors master a role. As if by magic, they transform into a character and sweep us up into their world. Skilled actors can so wholly inhabit an emotional state, nail an accent, or adopt the mannerisms of another era that we forget we are watching fiction. And that is the point. George Bernard Shaw wrote, "The function of the actor is to make the audience imagine for the moment that real things are happening to real people."

What tends to impress us most, though, is the sheer volume of text actors commit to memory: Shakespearean soliloquies; Edward Albee's raging dialogue; the long, beautiful musings of Tom Stoppard's prose; verse after verse of Sondheim's lyrics. How do they do it?

Off stage, I use and teach a number of techniques to help non-actors better remember names and faces, scripts and speeches, and facts and figures. But off-stage memory work doesn't require the same sort of physical and emotional intensity as, say, the lead in *Hedwig and the Angry Inch.*

How do they prepare? I wanted to know how they tackled especially challenging roles with dense dialogue and non-sequiturs, how they got back on track when their minds went blank, and how their training and experience shaped their memorization process overall. And I vowed to start a series of interviews that night. With Colin Quinn. Whom I'd never met.

After the show, I dawdled in the lobby and bought Quinn's book, an anthology of stories that his show was based on. I wandered out onto the sidewalk toward the stage door. Well-wishing friends and family members of the star were being ushered in for private audiences. I felt like a fish out of water. I eased my anxiety by telling myself I would focus on congratulating Quinn for a very entertaining show, and just ask him to autograph my copy of his book.

The bouncer poked his head inside the stage door and told Quinn that there was one more person waiting to see him. Quinn opened the door and stepped out. He fixed my face with a quizzical "should-I-know-you?" expression. I stood up straighter, mustered my best disarming smile, firmly shook his hand, and stuttered out my interest in memorization.

To my relief, the conversation progressed more easily than I expected. I said I was asking prominent people in different professions—actors mostly—about how they memorized their material. I had already published a book on how to remember names and faces and pulled a copy out of my backpack and gave it to Quinn. We autographed each other's books, and he scrawled his email address in my copy. "Let me give this some thought," he said. "Email me, and I'll get back to you."

The next day, I wrote him an email and two weeks later, Colin wrote me back:

"Memorization to a comedian is important. Every comic has their own technique, I guess. Mine is to tape sets and listen to them before I go on. It's tedious, but it works pretty well. Every comic has tales of woe where they said something in a certain order, and they can't remember the little word that was not the punch line, but it made the joke work. It could even be a preposition. And you go, 'why doesn't that work anymore?' And it's lost forever. But most comics never really have a logical technique or order that's consistent, partly because we are ADD in my opinion, and partly because we became comedians because we don't like logic or rules or techniques."

In just 125 words, Quinn's answers delivered mind-opening insights, a spirit of collaboration, and the shape of questions to come.

That exchange became the first installment of a blog that I'd build out every few weeks. Whenever I would go to a show, I carried a reporter's notepad with me for impromptu stage door interviews, as well as a copy of my memory book to give away as a token of appreciation.

Actors usually gave me their time, along with an email address or phone number for more detailed follow-up. Their generosity exceeded my expectations. They weren't used to discussing this topic at all, let alone with an anonymous audience member at the stage door. They let loose with wild, engaging, and very personal stories.

Three years later, I had amassed an extensive collection of interviews with actors, singers, musicians, improvisers, and professionals in related fields, all talking about their experiences with memory and memorization. The interviews with the performing artists comprise this book.

If you act, the interviews offer you a chance to learn new approaches or reinforce what you already know. If you sing, recite poetry, or tell stories on stage, the applications are also clear. If you are a playwright, songwriter, or script doctor, the knowledge contained in this book can make your words flow more smoothly, your logic cohere, and your themes resonate more deeply with both the actors and the audience.

But what about the rest of us? Why should we care? Understanding how performers internalize their roles can reshape our own learning process. Acting methods show us the way to get any material into our body—to know it by heart, down to our fingertips, like the back of our hand.

On and off stage, most of us are pursuing the same goals of mental clarity, physical expressiveness, and more intimate engagement with others. No matter what we aspire to become—a character in a play or a more enlightened person in real life—the lesson is this: the most effective tactics involve physical, psychological, emotional, and even spiritual immersion (Bree Elrod).

The same techniques that guide actors in embodying a character can help the non-actor master a foreign language (Joseph Medeiros), reconstruct the order of historical events (Denise Summerford), or memorize the periodic table (Mick Lynch). We can sharpen our hearing and our awareness of our surroundings (Chris Sams) to create more vivid associations. Our appreciation for the power of language grows (Rocco dal

Vera), as does our empathy. By being more present and engaged, we remember more.

Some performers will say that real life makes them nervous, that they can relax only on stage. This will seem contradictory to non-actors since most of us are terrified of public speaking. You will come to understand the value of breathing and what to do with your hands (Michael Rhodes), and how staying calm—and curious—strengthens your recall (Greg Skura).

For anyone who's struggled with dyslexia, it will come as a welcome surprise that a number of talented actors have figured out how to compensate for their learning differences to commit material to memory (Phillip Boykin).

When actors forget their lines, what do they do? The actors here explain how they get back on track, often without the audience even realizing anything went awry (Kendal Hartse).

What are the pros and cons of technology as it relates to memory? There are new apps that can facilitate line learning in context (David Josefsberg) and technology that interferes with our ability to remain present (Patricia Ryan Madson).

Lastly, let's not forget the value of old-fashioned hard work. Repetition and frequency contribute to muscle memory (Kelley Curran) and etch deep grooves into our consciousness.

The instructions for using this book are simple. Start anywhere. Jump around. Embrace the contradictions. Discover what approaches work best for you in different situations. As the actors here remind us, stay open to new interpretations, attack your fear of getting things wrong, and remember that when you get bad choices out of the way, you clear the path for better ones.

SCAFFOLDING

1.

*How Master Storyteller Jonathan Kruk
Brings Classic Tales to Life*

2.

*Nate Miller Walks Us Through His
"Memory House"*

3.

*How Denise Summerford Conquered
a 56-page Monologue*

1.

HOW MASTER STORYTELLER JONATHAN KRUK BRINGS CLASSIC TALES TO LIFE

November 2015

To conjure up his tales, a veteran yarn spinner relies on the "Story Train," the magic of threes, and alliterative pictures.

Jonathan Kruk is an award-winning storyteller for children who gives more than 250 performances and workshops annually at schools, libraries, and festivals. Using varied voices, creative dramatics, and language of the senses, his shows feature heroes of the Hudson Valley, Greek mythology, and classic fairy tales. Jonathan's masterful enactments inspire active listening, vivid imagining, and overall memorable experiences.

BRENT: How did you get started in your storytelling career?

JONATHAN: My kid brother was notoriously rambunctious at bedtime. I'd tell him stories to get him to settle down. We started out life in El Paso, Texas, which is the land of tall tales and daydreams.

BRENT: And you were raised in Westchester County, so you discovered the performing arts culture of New York City a short train ride away.

JONATHAN: Precisely. Some friends got me a gig entertaining at Abingdon Square Park in the middle of New York City. When kids would abandon the monkey bars, cyclone sprinkler, and ice-cream truck to listen to me tell stories, I knew I'd found my career calling.

BRENT: How do you go about memorizing all the details of the stories you tell?

JONATHAN: I begin with the story's end. I envision the story as a train being pulled along by an engine consisting of the conflict or problem to be resolved. The story events become cars; the climax is the caboose.

BRENT: What an evocative image! Give us an example.

JONATHAN: Imagine the story is Cinderella. The engine turns into the plight of the one-day princess. In the first car, I see Cindy cleaning, scrubbing, and serving the stepsisters. Threes are magic in remembering details and for resonating with audiences.

BRENT: Right, the Rule of Three. Comedians often use that to set up jokes.

JONATHAN: Next, comes the invite to the ball and readying the gowns. The stepsisters' gowns provide a visual bridge to the fairy godmother. I'll picture a gown on a godmother to make the transition to the next chapter in the tale. Again, I limit the godmother's wishing to three items. I'm seeing rats and mice pushing through a pumpkin shell: ratty horses, and mousy coachman, plus pumpkin carriage. The pumpkin takes the princess-to-be to the prince. I picture him giving three distinct frowns on his receiving line. His droopy mouth bridges to him dancing, only with Cindy.

BRENT: I love the way you visually link these elements together in a chain.

JONATHAN: On rides the train, powered by the problem to resolve, and the track consists of series of images and alliterative words.

BRENT: Do you ever write the stories out by hand for added reinforcement?

JONATHAN: I review lining up the pictures and words in order. I try to avoid writing things down. This forces me to rely on the mental pictures and words. If I do write, I wind up picturing my actual notes.

BRENT: Interesting. How much of your storytelling is improvised versus scripted?

JONATHAN: My stories always are structured improvisational pieces. Each telling differs from the previous, in subtle ways. Again, I rely on the "story train," the magic of threes, and alliterative pictures.

BRENT: How do your costumes or props serve as memory cues?

JONATHAN: My costumes truly snap me into character and turn on the story. I can perform "The Legend of Sleepy Hollow" without my 1790 frock coat and breeches, but it lacks the charm and nuance compared to when I'm wearing the garb. For example, at the end of "The Legend," I hint that Ichabod Crane "may have suffered a fate worse than a chase by a headless goblin; that is [grip lapel dramatically], he became a New York City lawyer!" I need to grip the long lapel of my frock coat to get the pause for the coming laugh, as well as give myself a physical cue.

BRENT: I know that hats are also an important part of your wardrobe.

JONATHAN: Indeed, changing hats in "The Legend" puts in my head the character voice I'm to use. When performing *A Christmas Carol,* how I hold the hat right before turning into one of the 30 plus characters helps launch each one.

BRENT: Do you have a colorful story about committing an especially elaborate story to memory or recovering from forgetting your lines?

JONATHAN: Many times when I am very tired, fatigue forces me to leap ahead. I must be on track when describing the barn dance to Ichabod Crane's race with the ghost to the church. I may wind up saying the fiddler brought music from heaven into the "church" when I should have said "barn." I'll back-pedal and say something like, "Well, the fiddler turned the barn into a church full of music." Most of the time, however, pretending you meant to say the right thing convinces the audience subliminally to hear the right thing. This does not always work.

BRENT: How so?

JONATHAN: Once upon a time, while performing an original story for a family audience about a boy who loved dinosaurs, I got in too deep. I'd contrived a wonderful series of ways the boy wore everything dinosaurs. I went head to toe: a Triceratops cap, a Big Al the Allosaurus image on his sweatshirt, Plesiosaurus pants, and Stegosaurus sneakers complete with spikes on the tongue. He even sported "socko-don" socks and "underwearasaurus"! I got into a routine of saying his head got topped by the Triceratops cap, chest by the big Allosaurus, etc. This flowed right into an easy prefacing for the underwear. I actually said, "The boy who loved dinosaurs wore over his 'penisaurus' underwearasaurus!"

BRENT: Yikes! What happened after that?

JONATHAN: It took a moment, but parents and kids looked stunned and laughed themselves out of their chairs. I still have friends who were there twenty years ago laughing over my slip!

BRENT: Congratulate yourself on creating a story that people still recall twenty years later. Thank you for being so generous with your storytelling!

JONATHAN: Thanks for your interest!

2.

NATE MILLER WALKS US THROUGH HIS "MEMORY HOUSE"

November 2015

A stage actor drives home the importance of listening on stage and seeing with the mind's eye.

Juilliard graduate Nate Miller is an actor, producer, and founding member of the troupe Lesser America. He and I talked in the lobby after a performance of David Lindsay-Abaire's dark comedy *Ripcord* at Manhattan Theater Club.

BRENT: Thanks for taking the time to speak with me. What was your favorite role when you were at Juilliard?

NATE: I played Romeo in college. I remember thinking that the second half of the play was a lot easier. During the first scenes, you're still figuring out the process. But you get into the rhythm. The more you do, the better you get. It's all about repetition.

BRENT: Have you ever blanked on your lines?

NATE: Oh, sure. Everybody does at some point. It usually happens if I get distracted by something. I bring myself back, remember where I am, and the line comes back to me.

BRENT: Right, take a deep breath and get centered. If you're playing a scene with other actors, they can give you a cue. Actors generally know each other's lines about as well as their own.

NATE: I know everyone else's lines but not because I tried to. It just happens when you get into character. And knowing other characters' lines came in handy in a later production of *Romeo and Juliet* with Actors Theatre of Louisville when I played Mercutio.

BRENT: So on stage you're listening as much as you're speaking.

NATE: Oh, yes! In fact, in the last play I did at Manhattan Theatre Club, *Of Good Stock* by Melissa Ross, listening was critical. Some scenes appeared chaotic, with people all talking at once. It required a heightened sense of timing and lots of listening.

BRENT: That's quite a change from the measured iambic pentameter of Shakespeare. Tell me about how you have committed more disjointed monologues to memory.

NATE: There is a visualization technique I've used a few times to help memorize complicated monologues. One in particular was when I played Wesley in Sam Shepard's *The Curse of The Starving Class* at the Wilma Theater in Philly. At the beginning of the play, Wesley gives a rather long and intense stream of consciousness monologue, seemingly to the audience. It is full of imagery and fragments of sentences. At times, it feels like beat poetry, and at others it seems like the scene directions in a screenplay. I really wanted it to flow quickly, as though you were experiencing the thought hurricane that Wesley was going through.

BRENT: So, what did you do?

NATE: So, I employed the technique of building a Memory House. I pictured my childhood home and entered from the front door and walked all through the house, placing each image and thought in rooms along my path. It was extremely helpful for me to mentally walk through my own home and recall the lines based on images in my imagination that were in a specific order. I still know that monologue because of this technique.

BRENT: Such an elegant method. In my day, we referred to it as a Memory Palace. I guess the real estate market has changed!

NATE: Ha! Well, no matter what you call it, it's still very much alive. In fact, the technique of building a Memory House is featured in a scene in Caryl Churchill's *Love and Information,* which I was lucky enough to do the New York premiere of at New York Theatre Workshop. We actually explored the technique on stage every night, which was super fun.

BRENT: You lead a very charmed actor's life, Nate. I wish you continuing success and enjoyment.

NATE: Thank you! I hope this was helpful.

Often asked why he chose acting as his career, Nate has a ready reply that is both eloquent and visceral: "People need art. Not simply for escape *from* their daily lives; rather, they need art so that they can *live* their daily lives. Art is the catharsis we experience without deadly consequence; it is the embarrassment we feel without shame; it is the pain that leaves no scar and the lie that allows us to face the truth."

HOW DENISE SUMMERFORD CONQUERED A 56-PAGE MONOLOGUE

October 2015

How did this actress use a technique invented by the ancient Greeks to memorize her material?

Drama Desk winner and Broadway actress Denise Summerford delivered a star-turn in *I Loved, I Lost, I Made Spaghetti*, a one-woman comedy about the madcap adventures of a single New Yorker looking for love while cooking a three-course dinner on stage. It ran at the Half Moon Theatre, at—appropriately enough—the Culinary Institute of America in Hyde Park, NY.

BRENT: How excited were you to take on this role?

DENISE: When the theater's executive director asked me to do this show, my initial reaction was, *"No way!"* It's much easier with a musical or in a play with other characters because you are on a team and are reacting and speaking in response to someone else. How would I even begin to memorize one big 56-page monologue, and then perform it while making antipasti and pasta—from scratch, no less!—with audience members on stage?

BRENT: It does seem a bit like scaling Mount Everest.

DENISE: Memorizing a one-person show is just not fun. In everybody's job there's always some piece of it that you loathe. For me, it's the tedious process of memorization. If it's a musical, it's so much easier, as there is usually choreography to help with the lines or lyrics. Or, in a play with other characters, your line usually comes in response to someone else's.

With a one-character piece, it's just you! This is just new to me, so I'm not used to working in this way.

BRENT: No question that prose is often harder to memorize than verse or music. The rhythm, rhymes, melodies, and physical movement help. So, what have you tried?

DENISE: My process is usually very calculated. I figure out how many pages I need to memorize and when I need to be off book by. Then I divide it up by sections, or little chapters, and figure out how many of them I need to memorize per day to be off book by my deadline.

BRENT: It can be tough to memorize in a vacuum.

DENISE: I've been trying different methods of memorizing, but I'm a very visual person and I like to attach physical business to what I'm saying to help in the memorization. So, once I get to connect the words with the pasta making and the other cooking, it will be much easier. I read and re-read the chapters over and over and try to attach it to something I will physically be doing in the play or something I can visualize or really "see" in my head. Sometimes, I'll even remember lines by where I was physically when I was studying them. Weird, right?

BRENT: Not at all. The ancient Greeks pioneered the idea of a Memory Palace They would associate consecutive ideas of a speech or script with a place they knew well, such as a house, public building, or park. They would do a mental walk-through of the space when they performed and reconstruct the content.

DENISE: This is fascinating! I love the term Memory Palace. Makes total sense, and that's what has always worked for me, but I never understood why.

BRENT: You can use physical locations on the stage or from your rehearsal space at home. Think of a sequential route through your house. Perhaps it's front porch to foyer to hallway to dining room and so on. Link each section of your monologue to that room in progression; you can even use fixtures and furniture as triggers for the details.

DENISE: I love it! I'm going to work with what you've suggested and see how it goes. It's so bizarre, but I always seem to blank at the same spots. So, transitions or a new thought that comes out of left field.

BRENT: Another way to link sections that don't flow together logically is by using your imagination in really absurd and visceral ways. Say you have three disjointed sections in this order: one is about a cat, another about cigarettes, and the last about getting a phone call. Link the cat to cigarettes in some crazy way—perhaps you "see" a cat as a hoodlum, sitting on a stoop, smoking a cigarette and up to no good. If the image makes you laugh or recoil, that's good! To link cigarettes to phone call, imagine that when you pick up the phone, a bundle of lit cigarettes jumps out of the receiver and burns your ear. You won't forget that sensation!

DENISE: Thank you for offering your help.

In a follow-up email, Denise let me know that "linking things together by using absurd images totally worked!" Marking up the script with annotations next to difficult transitions also helped. The act of writing and seeing the words on the page is good physical reinforcement.

CHARACTER

4.

KATE WETHERHEAD AND
GREG MULLAVEY EXPLAIN
THE RELATIONSHIP BETWEEN
MEMORIZATION AND CHARACTER

September 2015

Two Broadway actors discuss how getting into character helped them learn their lines for *Clever Little Lies* and other shows.

Award-winning actor Kate Wetherhead (*Legally Blonde, The Heidi Chronicles*) and movie and television veteran Greg Mullavey ("Mary Hartman, Mary Hartman"; "Hawaii Five-O"; "All in the Family"; "Bonanza"; "The Rockford Files") were starring Off-Broadway in a production of the poignant comedy *Clever Little Lies*. In a very impromptu stage door encounter, these stage veterans offered up insightful comments on the subject of internalizing dialogue.

BRENT: What is your technique for memorizing a script?

KATE: Hmm, I don't really have much of a memorization technique for just the words. The blocking helps a lot. That way, the physical language gets learned simultaneously with the lines. If the writing is good, it's easier to memorize because it makes sense.

GREG: Becoming trusting of the writing always works. You must memorize word by word, and the intention will reveal itself. Learning the other actors' lines as well as your own is also essential so that you know your cues.

KATE: I'm lucky with *Clever Little Lies*. Good writing makes my memorization job a lot easier.

BRENT: So memorization and being in character go hand in hand?

KATE: Absolutely. Once I understand what my objective is in a scene, then I know what my function is. When another character in this play reveals that they've had an affair, then my function is to become an investigative reporter. I look for the logic in the lines. Once I find it, the memorization goes very fast.

BRENT: What are some ways to get into character and out of your head?

GREG: The best books on the subject are *No Acting Please* by Eric Morris and *How to Stop Acting* by Harold Guskin. They show you how to get past any blocks and how to respond to the text. Big actors like Kevin Kline have worked with Guskin.

BRENT: Kate, you played the lead in *The Heidi Chronicles*. How did you master an especially lengthy monologue?

KATE: When I played Heidi at the Guthrie, I spent a lot of time sitting on my couch, learning the monologue section by section. I was driven by the internal logic of the character's emotional life, asking myself, "What would compel her to say these things?" I look for the justification, and the words follow.

BRENT: Greg, tell me about your experience doing Shakespeare.

GREG: I've been King Lear, and last year I played Titus Andronicus.

BRENT: Did the verse make the role easier to learn?

GREG: Good God, no! It was harder. It's a different language, not one you speak every day. Maybe if I were an Elizabethan, it would have been easier. I read the script over and over and over, and pretty soon the material just memorized itself. As the French say: la répétition, la répétition, la répétition.

BRENT: Thank you both for being so generous with your time.

KATE: You're welcome. Thanks for coming to the show.

GREG: Tell your friends!

5.

HOW BREE ELROD MEMORIZES LINES
THAT CHANGE NIGHTLY
November 2016

A master of character reveals her secrets of immersion...and the special meaning of a mix tape.

> Bree Elrod has appeared in several plays Off-Broadway, most notably in the one-woman show *My Name is Rachel Corrie*, under the direction of Alan Rickman. She has zigzagged around the country to perform in regional theater productions of *Angels in America, Our Town, The Marriage of Bette and Boo, A Streetcar Named Desire*, various Shakespearean works, and more. You may have seen her in the Martin Scorsese film *Shutter Island*, in which she played an intensely haunting mental patient. She took time out from rehearsals for *A Christmas Carol* at Kansas City Rep to talk with me by phone about how she fully inhabits her characters.

BRENT: When I interviewed the playwright Rinne Groff a couple of months back, she was insistent that you and I talk about memorization. Rinne told me about a 10-minute monologue that your character had in the middle of her play *Fire in Dreamland*. Apparently, the lines were rewritten almost nightly, and yet she says you mastered the new version every time without a hitch. How did you do it?

BREE: Let me first just say that Rinne Groff is a wonderful playwright, and learning her writing was an absolute treat. With each rewrite, Rinne explained clearly *why* she was altering things. Being an actor herself, Rinne said she understood the pressure of learning new material and assured me that she wouldn't be offended or heartbroken if I wasn't able to get all of the changes incorporated immediately. This greatly put me at ease and helped create a more relaxed and open space within me as I worked on incorporating her new text. I went over each change slowly and out loud several times and then got on my feet to "get them in my body." That definitely helped the memorization come more easily. The changes made so much sense.

BRENT: So, was this the most challenging role you've ever prepared for in terms of memorization?

BREE: The most challenging role I've ever prepared was the role of Rachel Corrie in *My Name is Rachel Corrie,* a one-woman show that jumps back and forth in time and space. I was fortunate enough to have Alan Rickman direct me in this show, and he was incredibly supportive as far as memorization was concerned. He knew learning a whole play was a large task and gave me the support and space I needed to find my way through.

BRENT: Wow, what a treat to work with someone of Rickman's caliber! What did you learn in that collaboration?

BREE: What helped me most technically in memorizing was breaking the script down into "bite-sized" sections. I started at the beginning and worked my way through the play a few pages at a time. As I worked, I broke down those pages into specific thoughts, beats, and objectives.

BRENT: Beautiful. Tell me more.

BREE: The more specific I could get, the easier it was to memorize the text. I wouldn't move on to the next pages until I felt I had a firm grasp on the few I was focusing on. Working on investigating a few pages at a time made the task of learning a whole play far less daunting. I learned as much text as I could each day, and when my brain started to feel sluggish, I stopped. I never wanted to push too much in at once.

BRENT: It's good to know your limits. How much does the content influence your process?

BREE: I should say on a related note that I find that learning good material is a heck of a lot easier than learning bad stuff. Great writing is a way of opening up your brain, saying to yourself that you need for it to go into your head and that you're excited for it to go into your head. I prefer to think of it as "learning" and not "memorizing." The lines actually go into my whole body; it's like flipping a switch.

BRENT: You do live and breathe your character! Do you ever use any visualization and association techniques to master your lines, or is memorization for you largely character-driven?

BREE: Sometimes. It really depends. I think my memorization work tends to be largely character-driven. If I understand why my character says what she/he/it says, then memorizing becomes far easier. I try to learn the thoughts, the ideas, and the words all at once. But I will say that sometimes thinking, "Oh there are three 'w' words in this upcoming line" can help when memorizing.

BRENT: Right, that's something Rinne brought up: that some playwrights will actually put sequential information in alphabetical order—like "deeply, madly, truly"—to help the actor out. What about the physicality of writing out your lines?

BREE: Sometimes I like to write out my lines. It helps me give focus to each word's significance (or insignificance) as I am memorizing. And I try to get on my feet as quickly as I can when learning lines, so I feel that I am getting the text into my whole body.

BRENT: Feeling the lines with your whole body is clearly fundamental for you.

BREE: I sometimes try to find gestures to investigate a word or feeling. I seldom end up using these in the performance, but it helps me explore the text, not just cerebrally, but physically as well. Basically, I like to use a variety of techniques so that the lines eventually become more than just "words" and "text"; they begin to feel that they are an integrated part of me. There are also recording apps that you can use to record the lines of the other characters in the scenes. That has been very useful to me.

BRENT: Indeed. The actor David Josefsberg told me about the app Rehearsal in his interview. It seems to be getting a lot of traction. Tell me, how do you keep your lines fresh in your head during the run of a show?

BREE: I try to go through my lines each day at some point before a performance. Often, during these casual solo run-throughs, I make discoveries about my character or the scene that I've missed during rehearsals.

BRENT: Rehearsals are a fascinating process. Another actor I spoke with, Michael Rhodes, said that "rehearsals are our chance to get it wrong, to get the bad choices out of the way, which eventually clears the path." To your point, it's an opportunity for new discoveries.

BREE: That's true. Also, going through the lines in this way assures me that all the words are indeed within me and that later I will be able to easily summon them and allow them to fall out in a spontaneous and interesting way. Well, that's the hope anyways!

BRENT: Even when you're in a straight play, I know that you use music to help you get into character. Can you speak to that?

BREE: I like to meditate before shows, as well as listen to music. I make musical mixers for my characters with songs that emotionally resonate with my character. There's this amazing part in a play I did where my character roars like a lion, so I put on some lion-themed music. It helped me get my mind on the place where the character is. The more you invest and stay curious, the better.

BRENT: And you went even further when you were in *A Streetcar Named Desire,* right?

BREE: Doing *Streetcar*, I immersed myself in a healthy way. I would get up, buy some Café du Monde coffee, listen to jazz...these things put me in the world where I needed to be—where my character was.

BRENT: Your brother Carson Elrod is also an actor. Do you each approach your work in the same way?

BREE: My brother and I have very different styles. We were in a Molière show together and came to our roles with very different approaches, even though we'd gone through the same theater program at NYU. He doesn't need back work or extraneous stuff; he just throws himself into the role. But I need more. For example, I'm playing Mrs. Cratchit in *A Christmas Carol,* and I want to know more about her back story. Who is she? What happened to her during her life that she became who she is?

BRENT: Well, thank you, Bree. It's been delightful talking with you. Your passion for your work is infectious. Acting is clearly in your blood.

BREE: I have to feel what I'm acting, and honor it. I put pressure on myself to do the best that I can. That's my job. Not I *have* to do this role, but I *get* to do this role.

6.

JASON O'CONNELL, A QUICK-CHANGE ARTIST WITH A PHOTOGRAPHIC MEMORY

December 2016

This master of disguise explains how comic books influence his ability to learn a role.

There's scarcely a Shakespearean play that Jason O'Connell has not appeared in, either in New York City or in theaters around the country: *Hamlet, The Taming of the Shrew, A Midsummer Night's Dream, Much Ado About Nothing, Love's Labour's Lost, Richard III*, and others. The mesmerizing thing about him is that he can go from playing clownish to somber to tyrannical in a heartbeat, as I saw him do in a production of *Sense & Sensibility*, based on the Jane Austen novel. The man is a quick-change artist who inhabits his characters with bottomless depth.

BRENT: What's the most challenging role you've ever prepared for in terms of memorization? How did you approach it?

JASON: The most challenging roles I've ever had to commit to memory were Hamlet and Don Juan (in Shaw's "Don Juan in Hell" from *Man and Superman*), but for different reasons.

BRENT: Let's start with Hamlet.

JASON: In the case of Hamlet, it was still relatively early in my career, and it was the first time in my experience that a director had asked—required, actually—that the cast be completely off book on Day 1.

BRENT: So, no script in hand at all. How did you react?

JASON: Having never done that before, I was nervous to say the least. I had always associated memorization with the repetition of working on a scene with the director and other actors, up on my feet, aware of the different circumstances and goals related to the production and the process. To memorize before having a chance to explore and play in that way felt daunting to me. And, of course, there's no bigger, scarier role to do so with. I was petrified.

BRENT: Being off book must have been daunting for everyone. How did the director support you?

JASON: Luckily for me, my director worked methodically and chronologically, *and* we were rehearsing in rep with several other plays, so we were only rehearsing three or four hours a day—as opposed to upwards of eight—so I was able to move scene by scene through the character's journey, committing perhaps a scene or two a day to memory before walking into rehearsal.

BRENT: Was it useful that you were working on a well-known play as opposed to something abstract and less familiar?

JASON: It certainly helped that the role was so famous. I think actors have more Shakespeare—and *Hamlet* in particular—embedded into their brains than they might think. It actually was a very civilized way to work, and while I feared that memorization without context might have led me to develop a "way" of speaking the speeches that might be difficult to break, I actually found playing Hamlet without *ever* holding a book in my hand to be incredibly freeing. I think I was probably all the better for it—though I have to admit, that is almost *never* the way I work on roles now.

BRENT: How interesting that this approach liberated more than constrained you. What about the role of Don Juan? What challenges did that present?

JASON: With Don Juan, it was a very short rehearsal process, and there were *huge* chunks of dense text—intellectual musings and rich philosophical arguments that often spanned pages without interruption. I not only had to learn it quickly, but I also had to make it feel natural and human, as opposed to a lecture on existentialism.

BRENT: Right, and no iambic pentameter to guide you. Sounds tougher than Shakespeare.

JASON: That was, in many ways, more difficult than Hamlet, but the approach was pretty much the same as it is for any great Shakespearean character—I needed to understand what I was saying first and foremost, and then find the emotional core of it all. I had to make sure there was a human connection there—a palpable need to communicate these thoughts.

BRENT: That you can immerse yourself in your character so quickly is a tremendous gift.

JASON: When you're on a deadline, it may feel as if there isn't enough time to delve that deep, but if I didn't, I don't think I could have memorized it. Learning things by rote is very difficult for me. Actually sitting with it and considering it and turning it over in my mind and heart was key even though the clock was ticking.

BRENT: Let me ask you about the recent production of *Sense & Sensibility* that you starred in alongside Kelley Curran. Though it was a relatively linear story, the staging had very involved blocking, with the actors themselves changing the sets around as they performed. How did you all keep the sequence of the scenes straight?

JASON: It is incredibly involved, and specific, and—in many instances— timed out within an inch of its life. It is also very dependent on everyone else on stage. Almost nothing happens without the company as a whole making it happen. The entire piece vibrates and hums as a result, even in its quieter moments. That's one of the amazing things about working with director Eric Tucker. You are always a part of what's happening in the space, and as a result, you basically have to memorize the physical life of the show the exact same way you memorize your lines for the show.

BRENT: All these components, then, have to cohere seamlessly into a single whole.

JASON: They are all pieces of one large puzzle. The show is both highly choreographed and yet pulsing with life. It's not mechanical. It breathes. The same was true of the five-person *Midsummer Night's Dream* I did with Eric last year. Each second you're on stage is filled with some role or function, to the point where you almost have to memorize the lines for the entire show—or, perhaps more accurately, an entire show's worth of information. Every time I get into previews of a show with Eric, I need a cheat sheet on my person, because there is so, so much that I—and all of us—are personally responsible for from the second the show begins! It's exhilarating and exhausting!

BRENT: I'm not surprised to hear you need a cheat sheet, given the organized chaos you're all swirling around in. On a related subject, in *Sense & Sensibility,* did anyone forget which scene came next or which character he or she was supposed to be? I always love to hear the creative ways that actors get back on track.

JASON: I think that with all the short, highly cinematic scenes that Kate Hamill has written into this very delicious script, it's probably easier early on—during previews, say—to get confused about which scene is coming up next or where your next appearance or costume change may be, etc. As far as the characters themselves, though, I think that once you've done the work and are up on that stage and those circumstances are unfolding around you, it's almost impossible to forget who you are in a given moment—even if you're playing two or more characters in a scene. I think the actor's instinct takes over. They may not be wearing the right vest or wig, but they can't help but wear the correct persona, the correct soul.

BRENT: Do you ever use any visualization and association techniques to master your lines, or is memorization for you largely character-driven?

JASON: It's funny, because my answer would be that it's generally character-driven, but yet I do tend to "see" the words when I'm first memorizing something. I don't know if what I'm about to say has anything to do with what you mean by the word "visualization," but here goes. When I was a child, I realized that I had something of a photographic memory.

BRENT: Now, that's intriguing! How did your photographic memory manifest itself?

JASON: I'm also a visual artist and for many years in my youth wanted to be a cartoonist. I even have a one-man show, *The Dork Knight,* about my love for comic-book superheroes in general, and Batman in particular, so I do tend to think of things in terms of images and even formatting on a page. Comic books are written and drawn very specifically with the aim to lead your eye to a certain point on the page in a very precise fashion, which I find fascinating. Sometimes the artwork leads the way in this, but very often it's the placement of the actual words, or word "balloons," on the page.

BRENT: So, does this visualization arise spontaneously, or do you have to use specific techniques?

JASON: I wouldn't say that I intentionally employ any specific techniques, but when I'm trying to learn something quickly—say for an audition, or just as a first attempt to get the book out of my hand in rehearsal—I will often "see" the page in my mind: the lines themselves, which words begin and end paragraphs, their placement on the page or in the book. I can visualize where the holes are for me. Where the peaks and valleys of the scene are. That all goes away for the most part once I know the words well, but I'm sure it's helpful in the short term. When I'm really steeping myself in a piece and am not faced with as tight a time constraint, the visual plays a much less significant role.

BRENT: That's why I remain a loyal fan of physical media—hardcover books, newspapers, magazines, paper scripts, etc. They contain so many cues—visual as well as tactile and even auditory and olfactory—to help with retention of the information. Any parting advice for my readers?

JASON: As with everything else in acting, there is no right way to do *anything*, so whichever memorization technique works best for you and allows you to get to the heart of the character is the one you should follow. And that will likely be different depending on the role, or the time frame you have to work on the role, or even where you are in your life at a particular moment while you are playing the role. As long as you're committed to the work and getting the results you want and need, anything is of value.

BRENT: One more question, since I know that you also perform stand-up and improv: if you know your character deeply enough, do you ever intentionally improvise in a scripted play?

JASON: I have had many opportunities in my career to improvise in scripted shows. I did a good bit of it in *Sense & Sensibility,* in fact. But I do so *only* when it is sanctioned by the playwright and/or the director. There is a big difference between a specific moment of improvisation in performance and a general attitude of sloppiness when it comes to the text as written. If you've memorized carefully, the latter shouldn't ever be an issue. I feel it's a privilege to be an actor and to speak great lines and thoughts and speeches, and so I really do try my very best to always be word-perfect unless I'm specifically asked to do otherwise.

BRENT: Thank you so much, Jason. You've let us in on so many ways of mastering material. I appreciate your generosity and look forward to seeing you on stage this month in *The Dork Knight.* Break a batwing!

JASON: Thank you, Brent!

7.

JOE CHISHOLM ON METHOD ACTING, MEMORIZATION, AND MOSCOW

September 2017

Atalented young actor shares his approach to character and reflections on his training in Moscow.

Some of Joe Chisholm's favorite roles he's performed at theaters in the US, London, and Moscow include Chris in *Miss Saigon*, Prince Eric in *The Little Mermaid*, Whizzer in *Falsettos*, Fredrick in *A Little Night Music*, and Orsino in *Twelfth Night*. When we met, Joe had just plunged into the role of Alex in the intimate three-man play *Afterglow*, having seen it once and rehearsed it twice. If you've ever wondered how actors master a role in record time, read on.

BRENT: What's the most challenging role you've ever prepared for in terms of memorization?

JOE: It was the last Off-Broadway play I did, *She Has A Name*. I stepped in last-minute and had a very compressed amount of time to learn a lead role in a 120-page two-act play. I needed to be off book for the first rehearsal. The stress was real. But I am the kind of person that performs best under pressure and in crunch time.

BRENT: What's your approach?

JOE: I memorize through repetition, from acting beat to the next, and then work backwards through a scene once I have it down. It's mind-numbing, but effective.

BRENT: Stepping in last minute seems to be a theme with you. You recently joined the cast of *Afterglow* to replace one of the three actors. How did you master the role of Alex so quickly? You told me you watched it once and had just two rehearsals!

JOE: I have a quick memory, and that helped me to pick up the lines fast. The beautiful thing about the human brain is that when necessity strikes, the organic mechanism adapts and steps up to meet those needs.

BRENT: Most people never have their minds put to the test like that—or flee from the opportunity. Does your memory work like this in other parts of your life?

JOE: Now, ask me my best friend's cell phone number, or even what day of the week it is, and I will draw a blank. But give me a three-page Shakespearean monologue and 45 minutes, and I'll get it learned.

BRENT: Different parts of the brain are involved with those types of information. That, and nobody bothers to learn phone numbers anymore. Tell me more about how you get into character.

JOE: My process when attacking a character tends toward old-school Stanislavski. It was the core of my training in London and Moscow. So, there is a lot of homework I do before stepping foot in a rehearsal studio, so when I walk in I can forget about all of it and just play. Specificity begets freedom.

BRENT: Having seen you transform into such a believable character, I'm not surprised you're a method actor. You seemed to grasp so deeply what drove your character and what he was after, and the emotion followed from there. And you internalize the lines through constant repetition, which you mentioned earlier.

JOE: In terms of line preparation, it is a lot of repetition. I have a nearly photographic memory, which can be a blessing and a curse, but it helps to absorb the lines quickly and allows me to then move on and focus on the character and relationships, which in turn solidify the line memorization. Once you know to whom you are speaking, why you are speaking to them, and what you want from them, then the lines tend to fall into place behind intention.

BRENT: You got your undergraduate degree in Musical Theater at the University of Cincinnati College–Conservatory of Music, which is known for its outstanding faculty, like Rocco dal Vera, who provided an interview as well. Then you trained in London and Moscow. Not many American actors these days get to do theater in Russia. What are your most memorable experiences?

JOE: This answer could go on forever. Moscow is an amazing place. Despite the horrific political atmosphere that rules the country, the people and culture themselves exist totally removed and unattached from the government's doings. The fascinating thing about Moscow is the sense of history there and within the people—the fact that these people have barely changed in the many centuries they have existed. Their strength and resilience are staggering. Russian culture has endured rather than evolved.

BRENT: "Endured rather than evolved." What a striking observation!

JOE: Their respect for the arts is one of the most incredible things I have ever witnessed. It is bone deep in their culture.

BRENT: Right, one thinks of the Hermitage Museum, Bolshoi Ballet, Chekov plays, and other high-profile commitments to the visual and performing arts.

JOE: Everyone knows Chekhov and goes to the theater and the ballet and opera. There will always be twenty-minute standing ovations where audience members bring bouquets of flowers to their favorite performers. It is a sense of love for the arts and a belief that art is the true backbone of their entire culture that is breathtaking and something I have never seen anywhere else in the world. It was inspiring beyond belief.

BRENT: Well, what a privilege to have that experience. You are truly gifted and fortunate. Thanks so much for sharing yourself with my readers. I wish you continuing success and look forward to seeing you again on stage.

JOE: Thanks, Brent!

RHYME, RHYTHM, AND SONG

8.

CAROLE SCHWEID ON USING RHYTHM TO OVERCOME THE (REHEARSAL) BLUES

February 2017

A member of the original Broadway cast of *A Chorus Line* uses a dance analogy to explain how she mastered a non-musical role.

Carole Schweid launched her acting career in New York City in the 1970s. A member of the original Broadway cast of *A Chorus Line*, Carole also worked with Broadway legends like Bob Fosse (in *Pippin*) and Shelley Winters (in *Minnie's Boys*, about the Marx Brothers' pushy stage mother). She's performed in regional productions of *Caroline, or Change, Cabaret; Over the River and Through the Woods; Crossing Delancey; The Tale of the Allergist's Wife; Broadway Bound;* and a one-woman play on the life and work of American choreographer Agnes de Mille at the National Portrait Gallery at the Smithsonian. She studied Theater at Boston University, has a BFA in Dance from Juilliard, and has directed over 100 short plays in her role as Artistic Director of Westport, Connecticut's popular lunchtime play-reading series, Play With Your Food—a brilliant name for a lunch and staged reading event. I had the good fortune to sit next to Carole in the audience at the play *Shows for Days* back in 2015, and we reconnected by phone.

CAROLE: My friend and I loved meeting you at *Shows for Days*. You asked me a Question about learning a role.

BRENT: Yes, I did.

CAROLE: Here's a story. I did a play last May at the Public in Maine, as the bubbe [the Jewish grandma] in *Crossing Delancey.*

BRENT: I loved the movie with Amy Irving. How did the play go?

CAROLE: To my distress, I had a really hard time nailing those lines. To be fair, I had just moved the week before, so I was tired.

BRENT: Fatigue and stress definitely influence memory.

CAROLE: But I worked on the play for weeks beforehand. I got into rehearsal and there were places where I just could not get it right. It was so frustrating. I'd go through the entire play before rehearsal, going over every scene.

BRENT: Did you run lines with anybody? Having a scene partner often helps.

CAROLE: I talked to my closest acting buddy every other day for consultation, a reality check, and support.

BRENT: Sounds like useful therapy. What did you do next?

CAROLE: Then I started writing out the part longhand. Finally that helped, with the lines and with the confidence.

BRENT: Great! Writing out the part is a wonderful technique, for both visual and physical reinforcement.

CAROLE: And then—the best help of all—was a speed-through rehearsal.

BRENT: Right, that's where all the actors perform the action at a faster rate—to help prevent the pacing from dragging. I know it's often used in comedies.

CAROLE: Right, and I realized that I was sort of playing the part in the wrong rhythm, that I was focusing so much on the words, that I was missing the play—or actually the rhythm of the play.

BRENT: What do you mean by that?

CAROLE: When you learn a dance, you might talk about the idea, or what the dance is about. But the first thing you do is learn the steps. Once you've learned the basic steps, you start practicing the steps together in phrases of movement. Then you put the phrases together and eventually, they add up to a dance—where each step leads to the next step, each phrase leads to the next phrase, and the whole dance adds up to something more than those separate steps. You want to learn the steps correctly, but that's not the overall goal.

BRENT: What a terrific analogy!

CAROLE: With *Crossing Delancey,* I think I got so fixated on the individual words that I almost forgot that the words, while important, are only parts of phrases, which are parts of longer thoughts that all add up to something. Once I remembered that it's not just about the words, I got on the right track. Then it was exhilarating. Pretty helpful, right?

BRENT: Absolutely! This must have improved your engagement with the other cast members.

CAROLE: As I became more aware of this, I started to get more and more out of rehearsing with the other actors. I started to relax and enjoy discovering the play as part of a group, instead of focusing on myself. Working on the play became a lot more fun. And the play got better.

BRENT: Makes perfect sense. I also want to be sure we have a chance to talk about your work with your lunchtime theater project.

CAROLE: Funny you should ask about memorizing because for over ten years now, I have been Co-founder and Artistic Director of a popular lunchtime play-reading series, Play With Your Food, where audiences come to see one-act plays read (but rehearsed) by professional actors—preceded by a buffet lunch and followed by a talk-back with the actors.

BRENT: It's such a smart name for a series! Your performances take place around Fairfield County, Connecticut, so you can draw some heavy-hitting stage actors from New York.

CAROLE: We have remarkable actors who come back over and over to Play With Your Food. I think the actors agree to do it because it's an opportunity to take on the challenge of a good play, while not having to invest the time into memorizing a part.

BRENT: Right. A number of actors, like Charles Busch, have told me that memorization can be "a chore and a bore." Others, like Bree Elrod, acknowledge that learning one's lines is just part of getting into character.

CAROLE: At a staged reading, especially for professionals who know how to use a script, there is so much freedom to express yourself, engage with the other actors, and follow your instincts. Done well, it's "opening night with a script in your hand," and can be a thrilling memorable experience for everyone.

BRENT: Elaborate on that. What do you mean "use a script"?

CAROLE: By "using a script" I mean actors hold a script in a way that their eyes can easily go back and forth from the script to the other actors with no extra moves. This is a skill that can be practiced, and like everything else, the more you do it, the better you get.

BRENT: What's the primary thing actors should know?

CAROLE: Be sure that scripts are held in such a way that actors do not cover their faces. This is also good practice for auditions, where you are expected to play a scene fully, but you also have the script in your hand.

BRENT: That's excellent advice for anyone who needs to deliver a presentation—don't hide behind your notes and remember to make eye contact with your audience. Any final words for our readers, Carole?

CAROLE: I have a theory—I think remembering has a lot to do with listening and taking things in.

BRENT: Good thought. An improv coach told me once to always listen more than you talk. I probably fail more often than I succeed, but just keeping that phrase in my head keeps me more in check. Thanks for your time, Carole!

CAROLE: Thank you! It's been fun to focus on this.

9.

JAZZ VIRTUOSO BENJI KAPLAN STEEPS HIMSELF IN THE CHARACTER OF HIS MUSIC

February 2017

A composer and performer of Brazilian-style jazz reveals the physical, psychological, and emotional immersion through which he learns his music.

Benji Kaplan is a guitarist, singer, composer, and arranger. Born in New York to a Cuban father of Russian-Jewish ancestry and an Austrian mother, Benji's musical tastes reflect—and amplify—his multiethnic lineage. His early interest in Afro-Cuban jazz grew into a deep fascination with a vibrant range of Brazilian musical styles. He began composing and writing lyrics in Portuguese while a university student in New York City. His musical influences include jazz greats, like Wes Montgomery, Sonny Rollins, and Lester Young, as well as Brazilian legends, such as Tom Jobim and Chico Buarque. In the last ten years, Benji has released three albums of solo and ensemble works.

BRENT: You are a true musical master—you play guitar, sing in multiple languages, compose your own works, and play both solo and with an ensemble. Does your learning process differ depending on the nature of the piece?

BENJI: Well, for me, the process varies not necessarily based on whether they are vocal or instrumental; each song is, in and of itself, a unique case. Oftentimes, if it's a vocal piece, I will learn the lyrics first. I will make sure I have them well memorized, and that I understand them and my relationship to them (which can change moment to moment, as we can always see new things). Then, I will get inside the melody and the pronunciation of the words, sounds, dynamics, phrasing, vowels, consonants, etc. Then, I will often start to learn the harmony, chords, and such with my guitar. Now I can put it together.

BRENT: You do exactly what actors do to internalize their lines, which is to explore their character's identity, emotional and psychological range, and back story. In your case, each song is a character. What comes next?

BENJI: There can even be a further step, which is to make the song my own, make it personal. This is where I begin to look for new colors, interpretations, sounds from playing through the basic chord structure enough times that I can begin to alter some harmony, do something that feels more personal to me to back my voice and sound.

BRENT: Beautiful! Does anything change when you sing in another language?

BENJI: The process is basically the same for me independent of it being English or some other language.

BRENT: What about performing solo versus with a band?

BENJI: When I perform solo, I have more freedom with stretching time and phrasing, both between my guitar and voice, but my preparation is essentially the same as with the band.

BRENT: Tell me more about how you collaborate with other musicians.

BENJI: With the band, you have in some ways less freedom, but you may learn new things from listening to the others. It can inspire different ideas, letting go and trusting in a communal situation, a challenge for sure, but strengthening. If I play alone, I can often significantly change the interpretation harmonically in ways that I can't with a group, especially if it's through composed music.

BRENT: Composed music meaning...?

BENJI: Meaning music that is arranged with specific melodic and harmonic ideas without any improv sections.

BRENT: Do you feel a difference between playing your own music and someone else's?

BENJI: When it's my own music, it always feels more personal to learn and perform than when it's someone else's song. I suppose one of the most interesting things is that I tend to remember and learn songs by making meaningful connections. The more a song speaks to me, the easier it might be to learn it, independent of its complexity.

BRENT: Say more about that.

BENJI: It could be an association to a lyric, the emotional impact of a chord on the guitar, or even the visual aspect, like the physical shape of a chord or line. It's a journey through many different ways of learning, making various connections: auditory, visual, etc. It's a story. Learning instrumental music is in this way very different from learning the melody in the voice when singing.

BRENT: What you describe vividly resembles the Memory Palace technique. Your music takes you on a trek through an imaginary landscape. Along the way, you see, hear, touch, and engage with benchmarks that make the progression memorable. Let me ask you, do you think there's something about the guitar, in particular, that lends itself to this sort of exploration?

BENJI: I should say the guitar is a very fascinating instrument, as you have so many odd shapes and juxtapositions. It's an instrument that really lends itself to a self-taught approach. In fact, so many guitarists are stubborn about learning rudiments, and theory, or even sight-reading. They would rather learn by ear. It's abstract and non-concrete, intuitive, spiritual, a tool, a guide—and a great friend or enemy depending on the day.

BRENT: When you have a piece with multiple verses, what techniques do you use to remember their order?

BENJI: I don't really have a technique for this. I just learn the song and practice it a bit more than other ones. It may take a bit longer to memorize, but once I got it down, it pretty much stays with me as with any other song of shorter length.

BRENT: When you play with a group, you have to know the styles of your fellow musicians, especially if improvisation is involved. Can you describe this interpersonal dynamic? Is it auditory, physical, visual, or something else altogether?

BENJI: Well, interestingly, it is definitely a mix of all three. The visual is especially key when say, for instance, a member of the band is finishing his or her solo and will want to cue this, so the other players receive this information and react accordingly. Another key reason for the visual connection is to deal with conducting a group; they need to know when to come in or what the tempo is, when to play the form of the music, and when to go into different sections, be they solos, shout choruses, tempo changes, etc. While this is true, it is at the same time equally as important to be constantly listening, as the visual cues alone aren't enough. To follow the musicians' groove and support their musical ideas—laying down a framework or a smooth path as an accompanist—makes the music more fun for the other players, generating more possibility in dynamics. And that's where the real magic can happen, together with knowing the form or structure of the song.

BRENT: Your words flow and twist like jazz itself. What about the physical aspect?

BENJI: I think it's also physical in that you feel things emotionally whether you are playing alone or with other musicians. In turn, those emotions can manifest themselves physically as pain, pleasure, anxiety, tension, excitement, maybe even embarrassment or shame, especially if the band didn't end the song together or someone suddenly blanked on the melody in the middle of the piece. But that never happens! Then there is also the vibration of sound that we are reacting to consciously or otherwise. That is certainly a physical experience.

BRENT: It's been a real jolt of energy to talk with you, Benji. You really feel your music deeply with all your senses, and that helps make it memorable to you and your listeners. Whenever I hear you play, it takes me to a higher plane.

BENJI: Thanks so much for reaching out. It's been a pleasure to think about these very thought-provoking, inspiring questions and ideas of memory and music.

10.

SINGER-SONGWRITER MICK LYNCH ON PATTERN FINDING

February 2017

This Irish entertainer with a golden voice tells how he memorizes cover songs, as well as the periodic table—for fun!

Mick Lynch is an Irish singer-songwriter from Dublin. He is a founding member, along with Kevin May, of the Irish band Storyman, previously called The Guggenheim Grotto, both of which enjoyed critical acclaim in the US and Ireland. He's also a friend and a regular at performing arts events in the Hudson Valley, where we both live. Mick can always be counted on to engage you with a story and put you at ease.

BRENT: When you write a new song, do you start with the melody or the lyrics?

MICK: I have always started with the melody and chords. In fact, I usually sit with a fully written song of melody and chords for up to two years!

BRENT: Well, no one can accuse you of rushing into things! How do the lyrics take shape?

MICK: The lyrics for me have to very much match the vibe I was going for with the musical mood, and these can take a while to come, to really find a good match. It is rare that lyrics come quickly for me.

BRENT: The fact that your material marinates for so long in your head probably means you have no trouble memorizing it.

MICK: Memorizing my own songs has never been a problem because I have sat with them for so long, and it's muscle memory.

BRENT: What about songs by others?

MICK: I struggle with cover songs, especially ones that I didn't grow up with. I actually do a couple of pub gigs as a sideline and have a big black book of all the cover song lyrics. Between not playing them that often and perhaps a beer or two while playing, it is important that I have them there to glance at. I will say that having the book has made me mentally lazy when it comes to memorizing. I should get off that crutch. Unfortunately for me, if I don't approach new cover songs with the initial intent to memorize, then it will be lost.

BRENT: There must be some songs that stand out more than others and are easier to remember.

MICK: Muscle memory does come into play, especially if I have forgotten the book. I have sometimes muddled through by literally going on instinct with phonetics. In fact, when I listen to songs, I never listen to lyrics. The phonetics for me are part of the music, and I'll only pay attention to them after a third listen or so.

BRENT: I've heard poets say this, that what drives memorization is the way the words feel in their mouth—the rhythm, the alliteration, the rhyme, and the meter. Your beautiful voice and unmistakable Irish accent make listeners as keenly aware of the sounds as of the meaning of the words.

MICK: My wife loves my voice but laughs at my inability sometimes to remember lyrics of cover songs. She calls me the "Cadillac with no gas."

BRENT: That's a charming way to phrase it! Tell me, what's the most difficult experience you've ever had memorizing a song?

MICK: As regards a particular song, the hardest song I ever had to do was as part of a theater production where I had to open and close the play with an a cappella version of a song by The Low Anthem called "Charlie Darwin." It's only two verses and a chorus:

Set the sails I feel the winds are stirring
Toward the bright horizon, set the way.
Cast your reckless dreams upon our Mayflower
A haven from the world and her decay.

And who could heed the words of Charlie Darwin
Fighting for a system built to fail,
Spooning water from their broken vessels
As far as I can see there is no land.

Oh my God, the water's all around us,
Oh my God, it's all around.

BRENT: It seems to have a logical flow, pun intended.

MICK: For some reason, it just was not intuitive to me. There are a lot of water/sea/sailing references that got jumbled together in my brain. Alliteration is minimal also, which can help phonetically.

BRENT: So what did you do?

MICK: I ended up taking the first letter of each line, STCH for the first verse, and remembering the word STITCH.

BRENT: Ah, an acrostic!

MICK: The second verse was harder, the "who" being an "h" sound followed by the "heed." I remembered HFSA. I can't even remember how I remembered that one! I really don't know why this was so unintuitive for me.

BRENT: It made sense to you. We can often remember our own nonsense since we created it.

MICK: I can remember it all now from muscle memory.

BRENT: What advice do you have for songwriters to make their songs memorable?

MICK: Oh man, if I knew that, I'd keep it to myself.

BRENT: We're all friends here! What works for you personally?

MICK: I am always drawn to alliteration. I use it a lot in lyrics like "It's time we talked" and "Money made you miss so much." It certainly helps with flow.

BRENT: OK, here's my favorite question to wrap up. What do you wish I had asked you?

MICK: To name all the elements!

BRENT: You mean, the whole periodic table?

MICK: I recently learned them by atomic number using a timeline story method with definite images for each element.

BRENT: The Memory Palace technique! Fantastic! Do you have a favorite association for any element in particular?

MICK: Molybdenum was my favorite. I pictured an ex-Liverpool footballer called Jan Molby (I switched the "by" around) standing in the center circle, wearing cut off denim shorts. If you see Jan Molby, you will understand why this is memorable.

BRENT: We'll let our readers look for him online. And while they're at it, they should seek out your official website to hear your debut solo album—"Aliens, Ghosts & Lovers"—and find out where you're performing next.

MICK: Thanks, Brent! I've enjoyed our chat.

BRENT: Same here. You are a natural-born storyteller.

11.

SERAPH BRASS ON THE VIRTUES OF
KNOWING YOUR PART BY HEART

May 2018

Members of this all-female brass ensemble reveal how they learn—and teach others—to memorize music.

Seraph Brass is a dynamic brass quintet (sometimes a sextet) composed of America's top female brass players. They are award winners of major competitions, hold faculty positions at colleges, and are passionately engaged in festivals and projects around the country. Their repertoire includes original transcriptions, newly commissioned works, and clever arrangements of well-known classics.

I had the immense pleasure of seeing them perform in April 2018 in Hudson, New York. After the concert, I spoke with some of them about how they master their parts. Mary Elizabeth Bowden (Trumpet), Jean Laurenz (Trumpet), Hana Beloglavec (Trombone), and Gretchen Renshaw James (Tuba/Euphonium) continued the conversation with me by email. Read on for wisdom that will benefit anyone learning to play an instrument.

BRENT: What are your reasons for wanting to memorize more of the music you perform? You mentioned that the music stands might be perceived as barriers even though you use them to great effect as props.

JEAN: Music stands not only create a physical barrier, but also, when you are facing your stand, you have less range of motion. When the music is memorized, the group can experiment with bell angle and choose to point directly at the audience or in towards each other for a softer effect. When the music is memorized, I also find it easier to connect to the group more frequently. When I know a piece enough to have it memorized, I can remove myself from the technical aspect and connect more, with my ears and eyes, to the music and the other ensemble members.

MARY: I personally like to perform as much by memory as possible. I think the connection to the music and audience is much more personal this way. For the group, we make a point to have our stands as low as possible. I have a lot of the show memorized anyway, and having the music as a reference is nice, but it is really important to not be dependent on it. Seraph Brass plans on incorporating more memory in our concerts beginning next season.

GRETCHEN: When we memorize music, it allows us to communicate even better and more constantly with one another. Memorization also allows for the possibility of moving around during pieces, which is a tool that we could utilize to highlight certain aspects of the music.

HANA: I think the memorization makes it easier for the audience to connect with us, and it makes it possible for us to do some of our choreography. Also, I think about the music differently when I have something really well memorized, so it's a different performance experience for me, too.

BRENT: When not performing, all of you teach music at institutions around the country. What memorization techniques do you teach your students to learn their parts?

MARY: I have students memorize melodies by being able to sing them using solfège [the "do-re-mi" scale notes]. I do this as well to memorize, singing the pitches while doing the fingerings on the trumpet. This is the most effective way for me. I also have students write out the piece a few times by memory. Learning the chord progressions is helpful, too.

GRETCHEN: I don't actually think of it as just memorization. Rather, I like to think of truly knowing a piece of music, and that includes knowing the relevant background information about the piece as well as the notes and rhythms. For me, this all comes from my conducting study. My most influential conducting teacher regularly conducted major symphonic works from memory, but the memorization of the score was never the goal—the goal was a complete and thorough knowledge of the piece, a knowledge that he used to make interpretive decisions about the music.

JEAN: I teach the "funnel effect": start by memorizing the general form and how your part fits in with the ensemble. Next, memorize melodic contour, followed by nuances.

HANA: Everybody is different, so I suggest to each student to figure out what works for them. For me personally, I think about the music structurally—chords, scales, etc.—and the patterns that my slide makes while I play; I almost envision a shape being drawn. Some of my students are able to memorize music simply through repetition, but I find I need to actively participate to make memorization happen.

BRENT: Can you elaborate on that?

HANA: Everyone is different, but with a student who struggles with repetition, I highly suggest memorizing very small amounts of music at a time, as well as looking at the music away from the instrument.

BRENT: What is the most challenging piece you've ever had to learn in terms of memorization? How did you master it?

HANA: I did memorize the Martin Ballade once for a competition. I had already performed it a couple times, which helped a lot, but I did what I said before and it helped! Twelve-tone is not super easy to remember. It's a great piece, and that helped! Also I got lucky and the judges didn't make me start somewhere in the middle.

MARY: I've memorized both the Jolivet Concertino and Tomasi Concerto. I used the same methods I mentioned earlier. If I can sing the piece using solfège, the memory falls into place. I also practice very slowly, so I learn to play by memory without ingraining mistakes. This is the most crucial part for me to achieve success with memory. I also practice difficult passages using different rhythms and also the fingerings left-handed.

RHYME, RHYTHM, AND SONG

GRETCHEN: Perhaps the most difficult piece I've had to memorize was the Tuba Concerto by Roland Szentpali. It's a wild piece and is just all over the place. Believe it or not, I did most of my memorization work on that piece while not actually playing the tuba but rather when I was on a treadmill or elliptical machine at the gym. I had my score and would "wind pattern" through small sections of the piece while practicing the fingerings.

BRENT: Explain what "wind pattern" is.

GRETCHEN: What I mean by wind pattern is that I would practice the breathing and articulations exactly as they appeared on the page while doing the fingerings. In essence, wind patterning is a way to practice your music while doing everything required in playing except making the lips buzz. So, I would wind pattern through a small section of the piece while looking at the music, then I would do the same thing several times without looking at the music. Over a couple of weeks of gym visits, I worked my way through the whole piece until I had it all memorized.

BRENT: That is an incredibly efficient use of your time, and it no doubt increased the cardio benefits of your workout! Jean, what about you?

JEAN: I memorized the Böhme Trumpet Concerto. I followed the steps I mentioned before, and I'd run through a movement in my head anytime I had to walk somewhere. I knew it was in my head when I could play it while thinking about something else, like watching television.

BRENT: Performers consistently tell me that they have lines, music, or movements running through their minds in their downtime. Anything else you'd like to add?

MARY: The more you play music by memory, the easier it becomes. Avoid labeling yourself as being "bad at memory." It's a skill like anything else that can be mastered.

BRENT: Exactly, it's just a matter of discipline and training.

HANA: Memorization isn't very comfortable for me still, but I'm learning a lot about myself through it! Once I had made a couple little errors in performance and noticed the world didn't collapse, I realized that I could let go and free myself up and I make fewer mistakes! And if I do make a mistake, it's less of a snowball/avalanche situation.

GRETCHEN: Playing in Seraph Brass has been the first experience I've had in memorizing music in the context of a chamber ensemble. Previously, I had been used to memorizing solo pieces—either as a tuba or euphonium player, or in my younger days, as a violinist or pianist. It feels a lot different to memorize solo music because you are almost always playing the melody, whereas chamber music, especially as the tuba player in a brass quintet, requires a different type of memorization because the function of the tuba in that setting is so different. There's also more pressure because there are five people working together with their music memorized, and we are all relying on each other to be rock solid on our parts to deliver a great performance.

BRENT: Thank you all for your time and insights. I greatly enjoyed your concert and look forward to seeing you on stage again.

GRETCHEN: You're welcome! Thanks for doing this!

12.

MEMORIZING SHAKESPEARE
WITH DANIEL SPECTOR
September 2015

A theater professor explains the relationship between rhyme, rhythm, and memory.

At a gathering of musical theater writers attending a workshop in the Hudson Valley, I had the good fortune to meet Daniel Spector, who teaches at the Tisch School of the Arts and has directed or coached actors in 35 productions of 25 Shakespeare plays. He generously shared his insights into memorization of the Bard's work.

BRENT: In Shakespeare's time, committing vast troves of literature to memory was quite common. Is that right?

DANIEL: I can tell you that Shakespeare and his contemporaries would have had hundreds of pages of material in their heads by the time they left grammar school.

BRENT: How did they retain it?

DANIEL: One of the major reasons why this was possible...and why it stuck... was because of rhythm: much of the literature studied was in some sort of poetic verse form. Rhythm helps—it's why we remember song and not prose passages.

BRENT: No question that rhythm and music serve as a memory aid. That's why children learn to sing their ABCs, and anyone who's seen *Mary Poppins* can remember a long word like "supercalifragilisticexpialidocious" by recalling the tune. But our memories are not perfect, as anyone who's ever argued with a friend over song lyrics knows.

DANIEL: Correct. In fact, there are "bootleg" copies of plays by Shakespeare and others because people would go to the theater and then run home and transcribe what they could remember, which usually wasn't perfect but also wasn't always bad.

BRENT: You mentioned that Shakespeare references this phenomenon in one of his best-known works.

DANIEL: Yes. There's a great moment in *Hamlet* where the actors arrive at Elsinore and Hamlet gushes to one of them about how he had seen him perform a while back. Hamlet then proceeds to recite the entire speech—which he'd heard once—from memory.

BRENT: Impressive!

One of Daniel's most treasured resources on this subject is *The Art of Memory* by Frances Yates, written in 1966. It begins with the ancient Greek orators, who handed their memorization methods down to the Romans, and continues through to the applied transformations by the Europeans—mystics in the Middle Ages and Renaissance and scientific philosophers in the seventeenth century.

PERFORMING ONE'S OWN WORK

13.

*Bilingual Actress Noni Stapleton on Making a
One-Person Show*

14.

*Charles Busch on Cabaret, Sondheim, and Acting
in His Own Plays*

13.

BILINGUAL ACTRESS NONI STAPLETON
ON MAKING A ONE-PERSON SHOW
Novembrer 2017

An Irish actress takes us through the process of writing and performing her one-woman show.

A stage and screen actress, playwright, and voiceover artist, Noni Stapleton is a force to be reckoned with. Noni recently wrapped up *Charolais*, a one-woman show she wrote and starred in Off-Broadway. Her character, Siobhan, wields a bloody meat cleaver that may have been used to off either a prized Charolais cow that her boyfriend cherishes or the domineering mother of said boyfriend. With her lilting Irish brogue, she keeps the audience in suspense until the end.

Noni shuttles back and forth between Dublin and New York for her acting and writing work. We were introduced in the Hudson Valley through the actor Michael Rhodes, with whom she has performed on stage.

BRENT: What's the most challenging role you've ever prepared for in terms of memorization?

NONI: I'm generally really lucky in that I don't have much difficulty in memorizing lines. The hardest roles I've had to prepare have actually been those that are badly written.

BRENT: That seems to be a recurring theme with other actors I've spoken to.

NONI: Well-written scripts naturally pay attention to intention and motivation. It's clear why you are saying what you are saying, so they are obviously easier to learn. A substantial part of the work is done for you.

BRENT: Of course. Some actors, like Jeremy Davidson, have told me it's easier to learn lines for the stage rather than the screen. Do you find that true?

NONI: When you get a part—usually odd TV or soap roles—they can sometimes feel very clunky and take way longer to go in. Plus, you have to learn screen lines in a vacuum. You generally don't get rehearsal time on set, so you have to have them off. I'm much quicker at learning lines than I am in rehearsals, so theater scripts go in very quickly.

BRENT: When you wrote *Charolais,* how much were you guided by the story you wanted to tell vs. the need to memorize it? Since it was your own work and there were no other actors, did you stick to the script or allow yourself to change the lines during the show's run?

NONI: I didn't give *any* consideration about the need to memorize it at all. It was all about the story and how to manipulate the audience. I was writing purely from my gut and am sure I was operating on the notion that "I am good at learning lines." So, yeah, I didn't give it a second thought. However, when I came to rehearsals, it proved one of the toughest parts I ever had to learn. Because I wrote it, I knew its rhythm. Every time I swapped a word or flipped a sentence, it would drive me mad, and I would stop myself in mid-flow.

BRENT: Charles Busch mentioned this as well. When you perform your own work, you're tempted to keep tinkering with it, and that can throw off your flow.

NONI: The way I learn lines is to figure out what I am doing in rehearsals and then they go in no bother. So when I kept stopping during the action, it meant I was taking way longer to figure out what I was doing. Consequently, it took an age to get it ingrained!

BRENT: At least it's a one-person show, so if you do improvise, it's not affecting other actors.

NONI: I am the only actor on stage, but I always stick to the script. The performance can change but the script is always the same—unless I mess up. But again, it's only a word or a line that might come out wrong. Then I'm back to what I wrote. Once or twice, something totally mad happens.

BRENT: Like what?

NONI: Two cows walked on stage at a festival I was performing at in Dingle in County Kerry (I was doing the play in a cattle mart). You have to react to what's actually happening. I believe I did improvise a line or two and possibly added some expletives on that occasion!

BRENT: Do you have a general process for learning a part, or does it depend on the role?

NONI: I always wait until I am in rehearsals before I learn any lines. Lots of directors want you to learn them and have them almost off before you step into the rehearsal room. I've learned over the years not to bother arguing anymore and to just do it my way. The lines go in in an instant when I have rehearsed the scene with another actor a few times because it is only then that I know what I am doing—and why I am doing it.

BRENT: You are bold! That must annoy the heck out of the directors. There is sense, though, in what you say. Learning the lines in the company of the actors in the physical space where you'll be performing has huge benefits.

NONI: Yes, sure I do a certain amount of "table work." But overthinking the part can lead to making decisions in a vacuum that you have to unlearn when you are making the play in a rehearsal room with other collaborators. The same is true for me if I try to learn the lines with no intention behind them. I can't do it. I always make decisions. What's the point of doing that in a room by myself? So what do I use? Repetition, I suppose. I rehearse them and they go in.

BRENT: Repetition is key. What about word play or visualization?

NONI: If I am tripping over a fiddly bit, then visualization can be helpful or making the associations. In *Charolais* there is a sequence that runs, "Poor her! How would she hold her head up? Hadn't she raised him better? His father would be ashamed." No matter what I did I always tripped over them until my director pointed out that the letter H was the link. "Poor HER, HOW would she...HADN'T she...HIS father..." As soon as I saw that link, I never fumbled it again.

BRENT: Awesome! Alliteration as an ally!

NONI: Also, sometimes memorization has lots to do with where I am on stage. I know what is coming next literally because of where I am or what change of lights or sound cues have taken place. If I forget my lines on stage, those factors can trigger them.

BRENT: Indeed. The ancient Greeks and Romans knew that connecting scripts and speeches to physical places is a powerful way to memorize. One actor, Nate Miller, told me about how he creates a memory palace. On another subject, I understand that you have performed in both English and Irish Gaelic. Does the nature of either language influence how you learn your part?

NONI: It's kind of difficult to explain, but I'd say mostly I operate the same way in Irish and English. Sometimes, though, 'cause I am not fluent in Irish, I have to learn the music of a phrase. Knowing what each word means won't be helpful, but getting the intention again is key because often the language is very lyrical.

BRENT: It sounds as though you've gotten more confident over time with Irish.

NONI: The first time I performed in Irish was terrifying. I wasn't entirely sure if something went wrong or if I forgot a line that I would be able to recover. So, I suppose I had to be word perfect out of terror. I did have friends and the other cast members run lines with me and stop me every time I got something wrong. Rehearsal, intention, repetition, and play—I think that is my method.

BRENT: Thank you so much for being so generous with your time and experience. You are a consummate storyteller.

NONI: Thank you! I hope this is helpful and makes sense!

14.

CHARLES BUSCH ON CABARET, SONDHEIM, AND ACTING IN HIS OWN PLAYS

September 2015

Actor, playwright, novelist, screenwriter, director, and drag legend Charles Busch holds forth on his loathe/hate relationship with memorization.

The multifaceted performing artist Charles Busch alit in the Hudson Valley on the national tour of his cabaret show *That Girl/That Boy*. He had lots to say about acting in his own plays, mastering Sondheim lyrics, and overcoming anxiety around memorization.

BRENT: For someone who performs in his own plays and interprets the works of others, memorization must be an integral part of your life.

CHARLES: Memorization is always a bore and a chore. I'm not that fast although I do find that it becomes easier the more often you do it.

BRENT: It must be less of a chore when you act in your own shows, though.

CHARLES: One would think that memorizing a role in a play you wrote would be easier. It's easier to get the gist of the role because you understand where it came from. The difficult part is not being lazy and paraphrasing and justifying it by thinking the new words are better. Ninety-five per cent of the time they are not.

BRENT: How do you ingrain the dialogue into your head?

CHARLES: I have two friends who are very skilled at running lines with me.

It's a real skill. That person must be tough but encouraging. Meticulous, but know when to nitpick and when it's better temporarily to get the essence of the line. I usually have at least three sessions with this person. I like going into rehearsal totally off book, so I can try and work on more important things, such as relating to my fellow actors and learning blocking and stage business. I don't think rehearsals should be about learning dialogue.

BRENT: Makes sense to focus on the relational dynamics. How do you approach song lyrics?

CHARLES: Song lyrics are hard for me. I can listen to a song five hundred times and not pick up a word. I type out the lyrics and study them like a monologue.

BRENT: You've begun incorporating Sondheim into your cabaret set. His lyrics are known for being especially dense and challenging.

CHARLES: I've always been afraid of Sondheim's lyrics, but recently I learned two ballads of his and found it remarkably easy. The thoughts flow so logically and the rhyming is, of course, so deft that it leads you to the next phrase. Mind you, I've never had to learn any of his patter songs. I don't think I could ever learn "The Worst Pies in London" and all the business with the rolling pin. That would send me to a sanitarium. However, as I said earlier, it's comforting that the more you have to memorize, the better you get at it. It's like a muscle that needs to be exercised.

BRENT: I couldn't agree with you more. One more question: has your mind ever gone blank in the middle of a set, and how did you recover?

CHARLES: I'm terrified of forgetting lines. In my cabaret act, I've had to let it go and just hope that I can come up with some gobbledygook replacement lyric and pray no one will notice. And my act is so casual, sometimes I just stop, make a joke about it, ask my accompanist to help me out, and start the song again. The audience seems to get a kick out of it.

BRENT: Smart move—stay in character and make it an opportunity for humor. Mistakes can be gifts. What about in a play?

CHARLES: I rarely go up in a play, but I have, and I get furious at myself. It seems to happen if I'm distracted by something an actor is doing that makes no sense to me. Or if the action has me rushing out onto the stage talking. I've gone through terrible periods of anxiety about forgetting lines, which becomes a self-fulfilling prophecy because you're not focused on the situation and life of the play.

BRENT: Right, it's critical to stay present. Thank you, Charles, for being so generous with your time and words.

CHARLES: A pleasure!

MONOLOGUES

15.

WHY MONOLOGUE EXPERT GLENN ALTERMAN PUTS MEANING BEFORE MEMORIZATION

December 2017

A playwright and acting coach offers invaluable advice for anyone engaged in public speaking.

Glenn Alterman is a multi-award-winning playwright, the author of 30 theater-related books (including 10 books of original monologues), a screenwriter, and a highly respected monologue/audition/acting coach, based in New York City. He was voted "Best Monologue/Audition Coach" by the readers of *Backstage Magazine* and "Best Monologue/Audition Coach" by *Theater Resources Magazine.* He holds the world record for being "The Author of The Most Published Original Monologues For Actors." His plays and monologues have appeared in over 40 best play, best short play, and best monologue anthologies. He offers invaluable tips for actors and non-actors alike about committing scripts and presentations to memory.

BRENT: How do you integrate memorization into your teaching?

GLENN: I've actually dealt with the subject of memorizing in two of my books, *The Perfect Audition Monologue* and the upcoming *The Best Monologues For Every Audition—And How To Prepare For Them!* There are several schools of thought on memorizing monologue material. For years I believed, like many actors, that the first thing you did with a new monologue was memorize the words by rote. Several teachers I trained with recommended that way to work. Now I feel differently.

BRENT: Why is that?

GLENN: Well, once you memorize your monologue, what happens is, to some degree, your final performance is somewhat "set." Even though you haven't sufficiently explored the meaning of the material, or even what the character is really trying to say, you've pre-set some of the results. By early memorizing, you cut out one of the most important parts of the rehearsal process, discovery.

BRENT: So, focus more on the meaning of the words rather than the actual words.

GLENN: I know that many actors prefer to memorize first to, as they say, "get the words out of the way." To me, the words *are* the way. The question I often ask my students is, "When you work on a new play, generally, would you go to the first rehearsal on the first day totally memorized?"

BRENT: I imagine they say "no."

GLENN: I realize that in some circumstances, this doesn't apply, such as summer stock, film, and TV work. Then why approach monologue material that way? A monologue is, after all, a piece of theater.

BRENT: No question. So how do you recommend actors initially approach a monologue?

GLENN: The brain memorizes in sections, patterns. When you memorize right at the start, some of how you'll be saying the words in performance is set. If you'll recall, when we were children, we were taught the Pledge of Allegiance. We memorized it by rote, the same way actors memorize their monologues. If you notice, we all say the Pledge of Allegiance exactly the same way. "I pledge allegiance...to the flag..." etc. Well to some degree, that's how monologues sound when memorized too soon—set, fixed. At auditions, you can quite often hear how an actor has memorized their material by the fixed way that they're performing it. There will be a certain unnatural quality to the performance. When actors work this way, that first you memorize the words, then somehow you add on the emotions, then layer on blocking, etc., it sounds like you're building a sandcastle, not rehearsing a monologue. Memorizing first is not an organic way to develop a role.

BRENT: This is why I get pushback from some students when they tell me they were taught *never* to memorize. I consider that a lazy gut reaction. What they were most likely told is that a monologue, speech, or script should never *sound* memorized. Character and context should drive memorization. How do you lay this out?

GLENN: What I suggest is that you rehearse your monologue, just like you would prepare for any other role in a play, in a step-by-step process of discovery.

BRENT: Does one size fit all?

GLENN: Actors work on new material in different ways. Some actors prefer to find the beats, the intentions, and the objectives first. Actors need to know, "Why am I saying this?" "To whom am I speaking?" "What do I want?" As they rehearse the monologue over and over, they'll discover who the character is and what's going on in that moment. And by rehearsing the material repeatedly, guess what? They'll discover that they've been memorizing it, too.

BRENT: Right, actors need to know the answers to these questions before moving forward. And repetition is always key! On a related subject, what are some notoriously challenging monologues? What makes them so, and how should actors approach them?

GLENN: Actors, mostly inexperienced actors, sometimes select monologues for auditions that make demands that are beyond their present skills and training. For instance, young actors who want to impress the casting director think that by doing a Shakespearean monologue, they'll get extra points.

BRENT: That sounds risky. How do you talk them down from doing a monologue they're not yet ready for?

GLENN: Doing Shakespeare or Molière or any of the great classics requires some knowledge of the style of the material. Doing it badly only works against you. I once had an actress bring in Queen Margaret's monologue for an audition from *Henry VI, Part 3,* where she laments the death of her son. This monologue was emotionally way beyond what this actress was ready to deliver. Add to that she had no classical training. It was sort of a train wreck. I had to gently suggest that this might not be the best material for her. Also, most (not all) agents prefer to see two contemporary monologues from plays with roles that you could be cast in. If your training and experience is primarily in classical theater, this might not necessarily be the case.

BRENT: When you write a play or monologue, how much do you think about how the actors will learn the text?

GLENN: I tend to write monologues and plays with dialogue that is both naturalistic and musical, and sometimes poetic. I feel that if the dialogue is honest, real, and easy to say, memorizing won't be too difficult. It's relatively rare when I'm in rehearsal with one of my plays that I hear an actor complain that memorizing the text has been a chore. I believe that the reason my books of original monologues are so popular is that they are "actor-friendly." I was and am an actor. I write for actors. I want my characters to say things in a way that feels natural.

BRENT: Have you ever made changes to a script because it was too difficult to memorize?

GLENN: I constantly change my dialogue when I'm in rehearsal with my plays, especially new ones. As the actors rehearse, I can hear what's working and what isn't. If I see an actor really struggling with some dialogue, we'll discuss what the problem is. If necessary, I will modify it if I have to. Sometimes the changes are just for that production, and sometimes it's permanent. If an actor is having difficulty with a section of dialogue, it's usually more difficult for them to memorize. If the words flow, if the thoughts are logical, they'll have an easier time of memorizing.

BRENT: When there is repetition of certain phrases, do you (or the actors) ever get confused about what particular line comes next?

GLENN: It shouldn't be confusing. Generally when something is repeated, there is a reason. It can be because there is an emotional build occurring, a miscommunication between the characters that needs clarifying, or a host of other reasons. If there is a logic as to why the words are being repeated, it shouldn't be confusing. It's really about the thoughts behind the words that need to be clear. If they're not, the actors and the audience will be perplexed.

BRENT: What else would you like my readers to know?

GLENN: I think it's terribly difficult to work on a monologue on your own. I know; I did it for years. It doesn't quite make sense. Part of you is trying to act, another part is trying to make sense of what you're saying, another part is directing yourself, and then there's the most damaging part—the self-judging that goes on when you're alone working on a monologue by yourself. Most actors tell me that they *hate* working on monologues. The solution is to work with a coach, or a director, or an acting teacher, or even another actor. That way you can just act the piece and let the observer give you (hopefully) helpful feedback.

BRENT: That's very reassuring advice.

GLENN: Another thing I've discovered is that performing the monologue (especially when you're still developing it) for your husband, wife, or significant other, if they're not in the business, can actually be detrimental to the best outcome. Since they're not theater-trained, their feedback could actually send you down a wrong path.

BRENT: That's interesting. I've heard the other side, too—that an untrained audience can offer objective feedback and let you know how your performance will play to the general public. But I get what you're saying.

GLENN: Because they don't communicate in actor terms, they will communicate generally or emotionally. I question if that's all that helpful. I believe because I still act and because I'm a playwright and the author of many books of original monologues, I am in a position of being able to help actors rehearse monologues and prepare for all auditions. I've sat in on many monologue auditions for playwrights and casting directors and listened to their comments. I've interviewed a great many of them for my books and always found their insights very helpful.

BRENT: Well, thank you, Glenn. You are a wealth of knowledge. I really appreciate your being so generous with your time and sharing your work with us. I hope my readers will go deeper and seek out your books and plays.

GLENN: Thanks so much!

16.

PRUDENCE WRIGHT HOLMES ON MEMORABLE MONOLOGUE AUDITIONS

June 2017

“The monologue detective" has three guidelines to help actors find and master the most suitable audition monologue.

Known as New York's most experienced monologue coach, Prudence Wright Holmes has been coaching actors for more than 25 years. Her teaching credits include Carnegie Mellon Drama Department, NYU Drama Department, The Actor's Studio at The New School, and The American Academy of Dramatic Arts. She's also appeared in films along-side such luminaries as Meryl Streep, George C. Scott, Maggie Smith, Annette Bening, Liam Neeson, and Whoopi Goldberg. Prudence has performed in numerous Off-Broadway shows, some written by others and others authored by herself.

BRENT: How do you integrate memorization into your teaching?

PRUDENCE: I offer various suggestions for memorization. Different students have different ways of memorizing. Some do it very mechanically, first one line, then add another, then back to the first and second and add a third, etc. Some like to learn it as they work on the character, so it happens organically; others like to listen to their lines on recording. Some hire a coach to help them memorize.

BRENT: Thank you for validating what I do! Some people get a quizzical look on their faces when I tell them I coach memorization. But back to you...what advice do you offer actors to have a successful monologue experience?

PRUDENCE: I think that three things have to happen in order for you to be successful in auditioning with monologues.

BRENT: A rule of three is in itself a memory device. What are your three?

PRUDENCE: Number one—you need to do a monologue they haven't heard five other people do that day.

BRENT: Very true. How does one find the right monologue?

PRUDENCE: I encourage you to be creative. Don't go to the tried and true monologues. Don't do yet another Hamlet or Tom from *The Glass Menagerie*. But, think outside the box. Do something that will really wake them up, that they have no preconceptions about.

BRENT: As "the monologue detective," where do you do your sleuthing work to find monologues that will stand out?

PRUDENCE: I've become very creative when it comes to finding monologues. I go to obscure sources like autobiographies, memoirs, magazine articles, newspaper articles, plays from other eras, independent films, even cookbooks!

BRENT: That makes me think of the memoir/cookbook that is Nora Ephron's *Heartburn*. What about trolling the Internet for material?

PRUDENCE: The Internet is a great resource. However, a lot of those people who create websites for monologues haven't really been out there auditioning with monologues, and they don't really know what's required. So, sometimes you can find good material on those websites, but it takes a lot of work, a lot of picking through hundreds of monologues. So, I think it's better to go off in directions that other people are not looking in, and to think outside the box.

BRENT: So, what are some sources that actors should avoid choosing monologues from?

PRUDENCE: *Spoon River Anthology, Butterflies Are Free, A Thousand Clowns, Glengarry Glen Ross, Fences, Who's Afraid of Virginia Woolf, Death of a Salesman, Angels in America...*and anything by Sam Shepard.

BRENT: Your website has an extensive list of "overused monologues," nicely classified by male and female roles—a very useful resource. What's rule number two?

PRUDENCE: Rule number two is, it's got to fit you like a glove. When I meet with my clients, before they come in, I send them a questionnaire, and I find out some information about them, which really leads me to finding monologues that are perfect for them.

BRENT: What do you like to know in advance?

PRUDENCE: I ask them questions like, "How do people describe your personality?" "Is there a role you've always wanted to play or people said you should play?" "Have you been compared to someone famous?" And "Do you have any issues in your life that you might like to have a monologue about?" You've heard the expression, "Write what you know." Well, I say act what you know because you will shine if you do that.

BRENT: Fantastic! So that's another reason not to go to the Internet. Your research leads to a much more educated answer. What is rule number three?

PRUDENCE: And number three, you have to act it brilliantly. Don't just go in there hoping it works. No. Thoroughly prepare for your monologue audition just as if you were doing a whole play. Read the play. Take notes on the character. Know who that character is when you walk in the door, so you're coming from some place.

BRENT: What are some things that make an audition memorable?

PRUDENCE: Having a strong moment before so that you come in in a heightened emotional state. What are you fighting for? Having very high stakes; having a strong beginning, middle, and end; really taking them on a roller coaster ride so that they remember you and want to call you back. If you do these things, you will have a really wonderful audition experience with a monologue.

BRENT: What are some notoriously challenging monologues? Why and how should actors approach them?

PRUDENCE: I think the most challenging ones are the ones that don't make sense, such as *The Bald Soprano* by Ionesco. In that case, you have to keep drilling.

BRENT: What else would you like my readers to know?

PRUDENCE: I've written four solo shows and memorized them all—a total of over 100 pages. It's easier to memorize when you're the author.

BRENT: Thank you so much for your time and knowledge, Prudence. You offer a very valuable service.

MUSCLE MEMORY
AND REPETITION

17.

TO REMEMBER, Q. SMITH WALKS THE WALK AND TALKS THE TALK

March 2017

A Broadway actress explains how hyperawareness of her environment helped her learn a role.

Q. Smith spoke with me after a performance of *Come From Away*, a smash hit on Broadway that puts a small Canadian town in the spotlight in the aftermath of the 9/11 terrorist attacks. Q. has toured with the North American Broadway production of *A Night With Janis Joplin*, playing the roles of Aretha Franklin and Nina Simone. She has shared the stage with such luminaries as Gladys Knight, Rita Coolidge, and Wynton Marsalis, and performed at Carnegie Hall, the Kennedy Center, and Barack Obama's inauguration. Q. is also a passionate educator, working to help children with behavioral problems and learning disabilities maintain their curriculum through the arts.

BRENT: What is the most challenging role you've tackled in terms of memorization?

Q.: *Come From Away* as a whole has been the most challenging by far. We are an ensemble. There are not necessarily any leads. The most challenging part of the entire experience was learning the sequence of events. The show is timed out physically and script-wise: the times and dates that the events occurred, which chair goes where for which plane set up, which character I am now, and on and on.

BRENT: So you're relying more on muscle memory. And your visual and spatial memory come into play more, too. It's not so much about the lines, is that right?

Q.: The lines weren't the difficult part. The lines only became tricky when the physical life or blocking of a character changed. I've never done a show like this. It requires your *everything*. I had no exact approach. If I tried one, it would fail or change due to the next scene or an added song or whatever.

BRENT: So what did you do?

Q.: I think what ultimately ended up happening was putting everything in my body and saying every move, every character, every line of song out loud when I'd rehearse by myself. It would go something like this.

BRENT: Shoot!

Q.: "It's Tuesday morning and I'm a Newfoundlander entering the coffee shop, which is stage left. I see my friends as they enter and I sing, 'Welcome to the land where the winters tried to kill us and we said...' Then I walk back to the table as a Newfoundlander. I turn around and put on my glasses because I am now Hannah, and I move stage left with my arms folded."

BRENT: Smart move! Narrating your moves reinforces the trajectory of the action. Speaking your movements aloud is also a good way for non-actors to remember where they place something they tend to forget—"I'm putting my car keys on the kitchen table so I won't forget them."

Q.: Ha! I feel your passion for what you do!

BRENT: Well, we can all learn from performing artists like you how to apply memorization to our daily lives. Another question. I assume that *Come From Away* underwent frequent rewrites, cuts, and additions. How did you keep track of the current version and scrub the old one?

Q.: It was hard with this one because they would cut it, then put it back a month later with a slight change—like *a word*. It would drive me crazy! But you just do it. It took a lot of focus. Still does.

BRENT: Anything in particular you want to mention?

Q.: There was a move that was cut where I had to grab a jacket for another actor to put on. After doing it over 250 times, they cut the move, but my body still does it!

BRENT: You teach as well as act. When you give master classes or run arts education workshops, what do you emphasize when teaching students how to learn their lines?

Q.: All of the things we've talked about—repetition, visualization, and character embodiment. Everyone learns differently. Right brain versus left brain, etc. *Come From Away* requires both sides of the brain. *Fully.* And at *all* times. I'm a right brain gal for sure! For students, I think the character embodiment works, and so does visualizing your actions. As I said, everyone learns differently.

BRENT: OK, here's my favorite final question: What do you wish I had asked you?

Q.: Hmmmm.....how do your body and brain react when you forget a line or a song? How do you get back in the scene? I don't know how to answer that question and am very curious how others respond.

BRENT: Every actor has been in that situation. A number of them I've spoken with have shared how they got back on track. Check out their interviews in this collection—Kendal Hartse, Michael Rhodes, Bree Elrod, James Miller, and many others.

Q.: This was wonderful! Thanks for being cool!

18.

HOW REPETITION AND CLARITY OF THOUGHT PAY OFF FOR JAKE EPSTEIN
May 2016

This handsome leading man shares his method for mastering constantly changing material in a Broadway musical.

Already a Broadway veteran at the age of 29, Jake Epstein originated the role of Gerry Goffin in the hit *Beautiful: The Carole King Musical*, starred as Peter Parker in *Spider-Man: Turn Off the Dark*, and toured with national productions of *Spring Awakening, American Idiot,* and *Billy Elliot.* A native of Canada, he's also known for his role as Craig Manning in that country's popular television series, "Degrassi." We talked after his performance in the recent Off-Broadway production of *Straight* and continued our conversation by email after his return to Toronto.

BRENT: Thanks so much for agreeing to answer some questions.

JAKE: You're welcome. I've been reading your book little by little, and I'm finding it all very fascinating.

BRENT: Well, thank you! Tell me, what is the most demanding role you ever had to prepare for in terms of memorization, and how did you do it?

JAKE: It's hard to remember exactly which role was the hardest to memorize, but probably memorizing Shakespeare in theatre school.

BRENT: Any play in particular?

JAKE: We did several Shakespeare plays, but I remember playing Macduff in *Macbeth* and having such a hard time remembering all of his lines. Performing Shakespeare can sometimes feel like you're speaking a different language unless you really take the time to fully understand everything you're saying.

BRENT: This is similar to what your *Straight* co-star Jenna Gavigan told me: you must be clear on what your character means to say.

JAKE: Yes, that was the key for me—clarity of thought helped me remember. When I spent the time to truly understand each line, then I found the memorization became much easier.

BRENT: Have you ever worked on a show with frequent rewrites, new material, and rearranged sequences?

JAKE: Before playing Gerry Goffin in *Beautiful: The Carole King Musical* on Broadway, we had an out-of-town tryout in San Francisco. The purpose of this is to work out all the kinks before heading to a less forgiving New York City. During previews, we were given new pages for every single show—and not just line changes, but completely rewritten scenes! We were even given a new second act one day and were expected to have it memorized and ready to go for the following night in front of a thousand people.

BRENT: How did you keep the most current version in your head?

JAKE: Keeping the latest draft fresh in my head was incredibly difficult! Luckily, my girlfriend flew into town to visit, and every night after the show she would help me memorize the new lines for the following evening. Repetition probably helped me the most.

BRENT: I remember learning that in an improv class, especially when making up song lyrics on the fly: "repetition is your friend, repetition is your friend."

JAKE: So true! I would just keep repeating the lines over and over and over until I knew them. I found it was easier to memorize when I had another person there to communicate with—very different from saying the lines to yourself in a mirror.

BRENT: Good point. We are social animals, and person-to-person experiences are still much more visceral and memorable.

JAKE: I don't know if got any better at the actual memorization, but I made sure to give myself the time to learn the lines; and usually, with a night's sleep, I'd wake up and know them a little bit better.

BRENT: What else can you tell me about the relationship between being in character and memorizing material?

JAKE: I always find it interesting that when a script is good, it's easy to memorize. But when the dialogue is awkward, not believable, and I don't connect to it, I find it impossible to memorize. Even though I like to repeat the lines over and over, I think that what I am actually trying to memorize are the thoughts the character has in the scene. If I know the thoughts, and know the lines well enough, then it's usually easy to learn. But when I don't understand or believe the thoughts, it's almost as if there's nothing my brain can latch onto. All of a sudden, the lines become just words, and not complete thoughts.

BRENT: I hear this often from actors, that being in character goes hand in hand with memorization. If you know your objective in a scene, that informs your function. And once you find the logic in the lines, memorization goes much faster.

JAKE: Well said.

BRENT: I'm grateful to Kate Wetherhead for that insight. It no doubt becomes second nature to professional actors like you. Thanks for being so generous with your time.

JAKE: It's been a pleasure.

19.

PHILLIP BOYKIN REVEALS HIS APPROACH TO MEMORIZATION

October 2015

The rumbling bass-baritone Phillip Boykin explains why he has an easier time remembering names than lyrics.

Phillip Boykin's majestic voice is an equally splendid vehicle for opera, Broadway, jazz, and gospel. He has toured the world with opera and theater companies and performed leading roles in works such as *The Rape of Lucrezia* and *Cosi Fan Tutte*, plus *Showboat, Porgy and Bess,* and *The Pirates of Penzance.* The bass-baritone had just wrapped up his appearance in the critically acclaimed revival of *On the Town.* We spoke after one of the show's final performances.

PHILLIP: You want to know how I memorize my lines? It's all auditory for me. I buy as many recordings and videos as I can, and I watch them all. As I listen to the recordings, I try to say each line before I hear it. When I can do that, I know it is sinking in.

BRENT: Anyone hearing you sing can tell that you fully embody the music. Do the words come as easily as the melodies?

PHILLIP: Not at all, I'm dyslexic. In school, I was a slow reader because I had to straighten out the letters. Now I write every line that I sing or say in a show, real big and real clear. I record myself singing the songs with a coach and saying each line on a recorder. It's the only thing I listen to until the performance. It's on repeat.

BRENT: The ritual of writing by hand, recording, listening, and repeating seems to be common among performers, whether dyslexic or not.

PHILLIP: I make sure I know what every word means and what it means to me. I try to understand why the writer chose the words he or she did, which usually tells me a lot about the character—where they are from and why they would say the word the writer chose.

BRENT: Keep going!

PHILLIP: I try to see a picture of what I'm saying, as if I'm watching a movie in my head. I feel the words with my articulators, and I feel the breath I use, and I use that muscle memory as well to remember what the lines feel like. I also use stage markers for remembering. I know that when I stand in a certain place, I say a certain line.

BRENT: In *On The Town,* the characters you play show up both on stage and out in the aisles, so you've got lots of locations to associate with your lines or lyrics.

PHILLIP: That's true.

BRENT: Here's a different question: how are you at remembering people's names?

PHILLIP: Now, names and faces, that's something I'm naturally good at! I think of something that sounds like the person's name, and that makes me remember it. For example, I know this guy named Will, and that sounds like "well."

BRENT: Like a wishing well?

PHILLIP: Exactly, a wishing well. I can picture that.

BRENT: And you link the image to the person, just like you link lines of dialogue to a physical place. My image for the name Phillip is a gas pump, since it's where you "fill up" your tank.

PHILLIP: I like it!

BRENT: Thank you so much for your time.

PHILLIP: Thank you for coming to the show!

Conjuring up an image for a name requires quick thinking. Actors often have stories about how quick thinking got them through a mishap on stage: forgotten lines, a costume malfunction, or something else. Phillip referred me to an article in *Playbill* magazine about a climactic fight scene in *Porgy and Bess* between his character, Crown, and his co-star, Norm Lewis, who played Porgy. One night, the knife with which Porgy is supposed to kill Crown "skittered into the orchestra pit." So he grabbed Porgy's cane, pulled it to his neck, and had Porgy choke him instead of stab him.

20.

WHAT APP HELPS DAVID JOSEFSBERG LEARN HIS LINES?

June 2016

A Broadway triple-threat shares his secrets for overcoming obstacles and mastering dialogue.

Singer, dancer, Elvis impersonator (in the musical *Honeymoon in Vegas*), and all-around funny guy David Josefsberg shares the stage with Sean Hayes and James Gleason in the Broadway comedy *An Act of God*. He plays Michael, a feisty angel who fearlessly harangues The Almighty for some of the crazy antics allowed to play out on earth. We talked at the stage door after one of the performances.

BRENT: Very fun to see you in tonight's show! Can I ask you a few questions? I'm a memorization coach and curious about how you remember your lines.

DAVID: Oh, jeez. I have a terrible fear of forgetting my lines.

BRENT: Really! You seem so confident up there on stage.

DAVID: I'm an actor!

BRENT: How could I forget! Tell me what you do to overcome your fearfulness.

DAVID: Drink a lot of bourbon! No! The truth is I usually prepare really well and know that my subconscious knows the words, even if I think I don't. Also, in a straight play like *An Act of God,* knowing what you are talking about and the ability to say something that gets you where you need to be is helpful as well. It doesn't have to be perfect!

BRENT: A lot of people think that memorization comes naturally to actors.

DAVID: Maybe to some, but not me. I have dyslexia; I even invert numbers. It must be genetic—my son and daughter are the same way.

BRENT: My interviews are revealing how widespread this is. It means you have to be more focused and disciplined in your work to get the payoff you want. Tell me, what's the most challenging role you've ever had to prepare for in terms of memorization?

DAVID: I would say a two-person play that I did called *An Infinite Ache!* It was an 80-minute show that had some scene work, but also huge monologues. I guess repetition was the key for me. I studied every night for a month before rehearsals started, and also had a lot of help from my wife. She would run lines with me as often as possible. Also, I would break it down into sections.

BRENT: That makes sense.

DAVID: If I have scenes spread out all over the place, I usually run each scene in my head before they come. Like the big monologue at the end of *An Act of God* I run three or four times before I start.

BRENT: Some actors I talk with record their lines, listen to them repeatedly, and recite them back.

DAVID: I've definitely done that—put stuff on tape, play it back, and break it down that way. There's an app for that now.

BRENT: Of course there is! I've actually heard of it. It's called Rehearsal, right? What does it offer that other methods don't?

DAVID: I have just started using the app, and the first audition I used it for, I booked. Rehearsal allows you to not only run the lines visually, but it also lets you listen to them over and over again. You can listen to the whole scene, and then cut your lines out for practice.

BRENT: So instead of juggling a digital recorder and a paper script, you've got the sound and screen consolidated. Sounds efficient but maybe not as physically engaging as hard copy.

DAVID: It's worked for me!

BRENT: Point made! You've been in musicals, too—*The Wedding Singer, Honeymoon in Vegas, Motown the Musical,* and lots of others. Are those lines easier for you to memorize?

DAVID: Absolutely! Musicals have rhythm. You're part of an ensemble and have the music and choreography to back you up.

BRENT: Last question—how are you at remembering people's names?

DAVID: Argh, I'm terrible at names! I've already forgotten yours!

BRENT: You're forgiven. It's Brent. Your mind is probably on overdrive after doing the show. Take a copy of my book; it will help you with names and faces, and even scripts.

DAVID: Thank you, Brent! I hope this was helpful!

BRENT: It was. It's been a real pleasure, David. Break a wing again tomorrow!

SPECIAL TECHNIQUES

21.

ROCCO DAL VERA ON VOICE TRAINING AS AN AID TO MEMORIZATION

August 2016

An author and professor explains how playing with pitch leads to improved mastery of scripts.

Rocco Dal Vera was the Head of the Division of Theatre Arts, Production and Arts Administration at College-Conservatory of Music in Cincinnati, where he specialized in voice and speech for actors. He was the author and editor of six books, many of which influenced curricular design at schools around the world. Rocco's voice can be heard on numerous commercials, and he worked on over 500 films and television shows, including *Raiders of the Lost Ark, The Gods Must Be Crazy,* "L. A. Law," "Hill Street Blues," and "Thirtysomething." Rocco possessed one of the most melodious voices I had ever had the pleasure of hearing. For that reason, it was also not surprising to learn that he was a trained hypnotist. We were introduced by a mutual friend and spoke by telephone. Sadly, Rocco passed away from a brain tumor in September 2017, but he leaves a rich legacy of knowledge.

ROCCO: What a cool thing that you have a memory blog. Boy, is that ever useful.

BRENT: Thanks for agreeing to speak with me. An actor I know who studied with you tells me that you use vocal exercises that aid in memorization.

ROCCO: I can certainly talk about some of the ways we—or at any rate, I—speak to actors about memorization. One special circumstance for actors is that we can't just recite or remember by rote. We have to coin and embody lines as if we are thinking of them for the very first time. That puts a special sort of requirement into the equation. It's all part of the fun—not said ironically!

BRENT: You wrote a 400-page book called *Voice: Onstage and Off* that captures your years of experience teaching voice training to actors. Among the hundreds of exercises, a former student of yours told me she remembers one that involves varying the pitch. What can you tell me about it?

ROCCO: Yes, the Pitch Isolation exercise was designed as a vocal technique. Its accidental output was that it also helped with memorization.

BRENT: How does it work?

ROCCO: The first thing the actor does is take a block of text and strip away all the punctuation and capital letters. What is left is a string of words, merely sound clusters.

BRENT: What comes next?

ROCCO: Actors must concentrate hard on what the voice does and always be mindful of pitch, tempo, and volume (also called intensity). In one version of this exercise, they must discipline themselves to keep the same pitch without varying the tempo or volume. They practice their lines by changing one variable and maintaining two constants.

BRENT: And that's harder than it sounds?

ROCCO: Yes, it is! When going higher in pitch, say, the tendency is to get faster and louder. When going lower in pitch, one must resist the impulse to get softer and go slower. High attention is required on the task. Low attention is required on the text. It forces the actor to focus on patterns of articulation and behavior.

BRENT: And you say that, as a side note, this exercise aids in memorization?

ROCCO: That is an extra benefit, yes. Even if the actor already knew the material, this exercise completely removes any prefabricated patterns of memorization. It hits the reset button, so to speak. Memorization emerges accidentally; the lines were in there, but the actors weren't fully mindful of how they sounded. Dialogue is not truthful or authentic if it sounds memorized.

[*Instructions for the Pitch Isolation exercise appear at the end of this interview. Also included are the variations with Tempo and Volume Isolation.*]

BRENT: I played classical flute pretty seriously in my younger days. Your description reminds me of the all the breathing and articulation exercises I did back then.

ROCCO: Very similar indeed! In theater, your voice is your instrument. Your whole body is, really. Our goal as voice teachers is to help actors do their job and bring out the best in them. One way to do that is through the mechanics of attention. What is it that you are setting out to do? What can you do with your voice to help accomplish that?

BRENT: Not surprisingly, you prescribe different approaches to memorization depending on the circumstances.

ROCCO: You know, actors have a lot of different contexts for memorization. They may receive word at the last minute that they have an audition that very day. Time is of the essence, and they have no partner to run lines with. In that case, the lines get stored in short-term memory. The rule here is essentially "repeat it until you can do it."

BRENT: And the process is different, of course, for longer, more complex texts.

ROCCO: Yes, many actors find that learning Shakespeare can be easier.

BRENT: Right, there's the rhyme, rhythm, meter, and structure that prose lacks.

ROCCO: Verse is better; there is a cadence to the speech. Actors become sensitized to the structure of the rhythm. And if there's music, so much the better. Those first few notes from the piano put you on more solid ground. And going back to the oral tradition in epic poetry, there was not only lots of meter, but sometimes a drummer for accompaniment—and reinforcement.

BRENT: Music definitely matters. It's why very young children learn the alphabet better when they sing it to the tune of "Twinkle, Twinkle Little Star." Let me ask you, though, about the internal logic of the text, the progressive thread of ideas or anchor words.

ROCCO: Ah, yes. There is a rational argument for memorization as well. What you call "anchor words," I refer to as "mapping." The term comes from my training in Neuro-linguistic Programming.

BRENT: Can you explain how mapping works?

ROCCO: For example, I might ask you, "What did you do last night?" Perhaps your answer is, "I made pasta."

BRENT: You mean, like, for real.

ROCCO: Yes, for real. If you actually made pasta last night, then, when recounting your story, you would visualize standing in your kitchen. You would know where the sink, stove, and fridge are. You might point to those spaces, move toward them, and recall the specific order of events. But if an actor's character made pasta...

BRENT: ...And that person him or herself didn't really do it...

ROCCO: ...Then the actor must "remember" these same physical spaces when recounting the imaginary episode or it will ring false. Actors can forget to do this. This holds true even for abstract concepts. If an actor must evoke truth, deceit, or affection, he or she must map those concepts to make them concrete.

BRENT: So, conjure up the world you were in when you experienced these emotions or performed certain actions.

ROCCO: Exactly! Map first, text second. The words follow the experience.

BRENT: This makes perfect sense. Humans fare much better with spatial and visual memory than with words.

ROCCO: Indeed we do. Still, as you know, people have different learning styles. Actors—everyone, really—needs to understand their own learning process: are they primarily visual, auditory, or kinesthetic?

BRENT: I've been lucky enough to have some teachers who knew how to make material accessible to all three groups. They would provide handouts, have us write on the chalkboard, get up and move around, and repeat aloud.

ROCCO: Those are very wise teachers. I encourage everyone to learn which style is best for them—*and* to know how to translate from one style to another to convey the concept to others. For example, if you are saying or writing the word "arrow," move your arm in a sweeping gesture.

BRENT: Speaking of styles, I once saw Sutton Foster do a cabaret show. She said that one of her techniques for mastering the nuances of a song was to sing it with different emotions—wistful, defiant, hopeful, etc. Approaching it from distinctive angles made her more aware of the flow and meaning. She had a bowl on stage with folded-up pieces of paper that had different adjectives written on them. She pulled one out at random and sang her next number in that vein.

ROCCO: That is so exposing! So vulnerable!

BRENT: She's a pro and made it look effortless, but I'm sure she took delight in the challenge.

ROCCO: How beautiful!

BRENT: Well, it has been really thrilling to talk with you. Anything else you would like to add?

ROCCO: Going back to memorization, I will say that when actors transition from stage to screen work, they lose the ability to memorize long stretches of text. Movies are shot scene by scene, and dialogue is learned in smaller chunks.

BRENT: Like an Olympic athlete who stops training so strenuously. Use it or lose it.

ROCCO: Yes, exactly. Memorizing for the stage can be fatiguing, but oh so rewarding.

BRENT: Thank you, Rocco. Your students are very fortunate to have such a knowledgeable and compassionate mentor. This has been incredibly enlightening for me.

ROCCO: You are very kind. Thank you so much. It was so fun talking to you. You are carving out an amazing sub-specialty. I look forward to reading your book!

The following exercises are used with permission from the second edition of Rocco Dal Vera's book *Voice: Onstage and Off.*

EXERCISE 2.9.2.1 PITCH ISOLATION

1. Use either your performance text or [dummy text from elsewhere]. Speak each syllable (not each word) separately at a clearly defined regular rate and volume. Start at your normal median note.

2. Maintaining rate and volume consistency, move the pitch upward away from your median note.

3. Step the pitch using regular intervals, never repeating any pitch, as high as your voice can go (be sure to explore way above the normal speaking

range, well into the falsetto range). When you are as high as you can go, step downward evenly to as low as you can, then return to your median note. You have completed one cycle.

4. Continue repeating this cycle as long as you like, or until you run out of text.

EXERCISE 2.6.1.1 TEMPO ISOLATION

1. Use either your performance text or [dummy text from elsewhere]. Speak each syllable (not each word) separately at a clearly defined regular tempo, keeping them all on the same pitch and at the same intensity. This will sound robotic.

2. Gradually increase the tempo until you are going as fast as you can articulate. Do not raise the pitch or volume.

3. As soon as you have reached maximum speed, smoothly begin to slow down, passing through your starting speed and becoming definitively slow. Do not drop the pitch or loudness.

4. Return to your original tempo. You have completed one cycle.

Hints: As you may suspect, this requires superior breath management. Don't break the rhythm to breathe. There will always be space for breath until you reach maximum speed. If you have a hard time maintaining a steady pitch, pick a pitch just above your normal note so you can hear it more distinctly. If you still have a problem, put someone on each side of you and have them hum the pitch in your ear to keep you on track.

EXERCISE 2.10.2.3 VOLUME ISOLATION

1. As with the other isolation exercises, use either your performance text or [dummy text from elsewhere].

2. Isolate loudness or intensity away from pitch and rate. One's natural

instinct is to raise pitch and increase speed as you get louder, and to do just the opposite when you get softer. Resist those impulses.

3. To find the easiest pitch for this exercise, shout "HEY!" as if you were calling to a friend in the next block. Listen carefully to the pitch you choose and say "hey" softly on the same pitch. This is your starting point. You may be surprised how high it seems.

4. Speak each syllable separately. Start at a conversational volume level, with each syllable slightly louder than the one before it, until you reach maximum level, then reverse the process, through a barely audible level back to normal, completing one cycle. Remember that throughout, the pitch and speed must remain constant.

5. Being wary of vocal fatigue, continue to repeat the cycle until you have gone through the full text. Watch for general body and neck tension and focus on keeping a clear, consistent tone throughout the full range from soft to loud.

22.

WHAT JAMES MILLER LEARNED FROM ROB LOWE AND ALLISON JANNEY

September 2016

A young actor offers practical advice on memorizing monologues and scene work.

Originally from Atlanta, Georgia, James Miller moved to New York about six years ago to pursue acting. Since then, he has studied at Stella Adler Studio, T. Schreiber Studio, and The Upright Citizens Brigade. His work has consisted of Off-Off-Off-Broadway theater and student (or otherwise minor) film productions. Remarkably self-aware and brimming with practical ideas from his studies, James is a very entertaining and instructive storyteller.

BRENT: What was the most challenging role you ever had to prepare for in terms of memorization?

JAMES: Probably the most difficult so far was a production of *Romeo and Juliet*, in which I played Friar Laurence. It was my first production of Shakespeare, and the friar has the third most lines in the play, even if we were pretty judicious in our cuts to the script. So, having a huge amount of lines, coupled with using the verse form for the first time, made for a pretty big challenge.

BRENT: Sounds like a very tall order! How did you tackle the role?

JAMES: Thankfully, I had recently read through Rob Lowe's second autobiography, *Love Life*. On page 167 of the hardcover edition, he details his process for memorizing lines, which he picked up from Allison

Janney when they worked together on "The West Wing," and which she had picked up from someone who studied at the Royal Shakespeare Company.

BRENT: You've got me intrigued. Keep going!

JAMES: It goes like this: Take a line you need to memorize, and write out just the first letter of each word. Include punctuation. For example, the line, "In sooth, I know not why I am so sad," would look like this: "I s, I k n w I a s s." This gives you a cue (the letter), while making your brain fill in the rest; you are prompted, but you also have to struggle. (I also keep the format of the text the same, i.e., either prose or verse.) After going through the process of writing out the letters of my lines, I then used the coded version for memorization, only using the script as a reference if I couldn't recall precisely what the letter stood for.

BRENT: Smart approach. Preserving the punctuation and capitalization, as well as the format, provides some useful hints. Do you also use this technique for scene work?

JAMES: While that technique works perfectly well on its own for monologues, for scene work I coupled Lowe's strategy with a technique I picked up at T. Schreiber Studio in New York. For any scenes, I made a recording of just the other person's lines, without emotion or performance, with three-second pauses in between. With this recording, I could hear the other person's lines, pause the recording to deliver my lines (also without emotion or performance, since this is purely technical and I didn't want to get stuck in interpretations), and then continued playing the recording for the next lines, pausing it when I needed to deliver my lines, and so on.

BRENT: Beautiful! A lot of actors tell me they know everyone else's lines as well as their own through osmosis, so it's wise to learn yours not just in isolation but also in the context of the show. How do you pace yourself to avoid overloading your brain?

JAMES: On top of that, I used a studying technique that helped me through college, where I memorize lines for 20 minutes, then rest for 10 minutes, before memorizing for another 20 minutes, and so on. I also tried to study right when I got up or right before going to bed, since I hear that is also helpful for memorization.

BRENT: No question that memorization can be as fatiguing as physical activity. Timing it with periods when your brain is the most alert, impressionable, or both is helpful. Anything else?

JAMES: I also broke up the script into chunks that I was memorizing, focusing on one long monologue or scene a day, so as not to get too overwhelmed by the task before me.

BRENT: What about commitment to your character? How does that help you learn your lines?

JAMES: Committing to character helps me memorize lines because if I understand my character, and more importantly, what my character is trying to achieve, I can parse out exactly what the character means with the lines he says, how they should be helping him to reach his objective, and, therefore, in what order the thoughts and lines should happen.

BRENT: Right, it's best to think about a monologue as a gradual progression of ideas, not as a monolithic mass.

JAMES: Almost no characters have giant monologues memorized and prepared to deliver to the other characters; each line is supposed to build on the one before it, and flow organically together, like dominoes falling one after the other. So, if I understand the point my character's trying to make, I can start to see the thought process my character is going through, which makes it easier to remember that my character is making a specific point with one line (or several), and then has a new point he builds on after that, and so on.

BRENT: Any examples from recent performances?

JAMES: A recent example was a one-act I was in last month. I was playing a NASA commander briefing a roomful of potential candidates for a mission to Mars. I had an enormous, ten-line run-on sentence to deliver during this introductory speech. It helped me to memorize it by recognizing that the character is walking them through the entire mission process, undercutting the likelihood of success at each stage, before finally making it clear that, ultimately, it wouldn't succeed because of the lack of commitment by the astronauts in the room.

BRENT: So the sequence of ideas made sense in your head.

JAMES: On the page it seems like a railing, unending sentence, but by figuring out why my character was saying what he was saying, it helped me recognize why he was constructing his sentences in a particular way, which helped to cement the lines in my head.

BRENT: The "why" almost always informs the "what" and puts you on a path of knowing where the thread of the monologue is going. Despite that preparation, has your mind ever gone blank on stage? How did you recover?

JAMES: I'm fairly certain every actor has gone up on his lines at some point or another; I'm no exception. I can think of two specific examples of me going up on my lines. The first was during a high school production of *Into the Woods*. I was playing the Baker, and it was the beginning of the second act. My character goes to Cinderella to warn them about the giant attacking the kingdom, and somehow I just completely forgot what my next lines were. I ended up just blurting out "Giant!" right into Cinderella's face, before stumbling over myself to get us back on track, which we eventually did.

BRENT: Oh my! Glad you recovered from it. What was your take-away from this experience?

JAMES: The important lesson I took away—aside from focusing and being off book as best as possible—is to grasp for the idea of what I'm supposed to be talking about, which will hopefully guide me back to the precise words written by the playwright.

BRENT: Have you ever been distracted by the audience to the point that it interfered with your performance?

JAMES: That happened with the one-act I recently mentioned. In that large monologue I just discussed memorizing, I went up on my lines right as I started the huge run-on sentence. It was the first time we'd performed the show in front of an audience, and I think their willingness to laugh at the humor sort of threw me off, to where I completely blanked on where I was in the script.

BRENT: How did you handle it?

JAMES: I took half a beat before launching into the speech, once again trying to grasp onto the idea of what I was talking about, and doing the best I could to land on the exact words. It meant I changed one important word—"rocket"—with another serviceable, if entirely inaccurate, word—"airship"—to get moving with the line I had blanked on.

BRENT: The important thing is that you got back on track. Well, thanks so much for your time, James. You've been very generous to share your stories and techniques with us. I wish you a long, successful career on stage.

JAMES: Thank you for involving me in your work!

23.

THOMAS E. SULLIVAN AND THE
POWER OF PRACTICAL AESTHETICS
May 2016

Abudding actor tells us how he keeps his focus, with a nod to David Mamet.

A recent graduate of NYU's Tisch School of the Arts, Thomas E. Sullivan received his drama training from the Atlantic Acting School. Making his Off-Broadway debut in the play *Straight*, Sullivan favorably impressed critics for his portrayal of the wisecracking Chris, the male love interest of the sexually ambivalent protagonist, Ben. We spoke after one of the final performances.

BRENT: What a treat! I've gotten to interview all three cast members of *Straight*—you, Jake Epstein, and Jenna Gavigan. This was your Off-Broadway debut, and *The New York Times* praised you for your slacker jokiness and sharp timing. That must have felt pretty good. Was Chris an easy part for you to learn?

TOM: Chris was a particularly challenging role for me in terms of memorization, primarily because the character speaks in a very modern way. His vernacular is not so dissimilar from my own, and I found it difficult to memorize in rehearsals for this reason.

BRENT: That's surprising. One would think the familiarity would make it easier, unlike, say, Shakespeare. How did you tackle this?

TOM: I usually sit down with a friend and just pace for hours and hours until I can go a whole scene without getting a word wrong, and this project was no exception. It took a long time to get everything down!

BRENT: I'll bet. You had some very long, moving passages, as well as some great comedic riffs. In my opinion, Chris has the funniest line in the play.

TOM: I'm guessing you mean, "Not every gay guy, like, burps glitter."

BRENT: Clever stuff! Chris has a very intense—and often infuriating—relationship with Ben, urging him to come clean about his sexuality. Some scenes generated a lot of emotional reaction from the audience in a small theater. How do you stay focused and tune out off-stage noise and distractions?

TOM: I utilize a technique called Practical Aesthetics, which keeps me focused exclusively on my scene partner while I'm onstage. In other words, I'm working to achieve a specific change in my scene partner.

BRENT: I've heard that David Mamet is a big proponent of this method. It's precisely what you say—identify what your character wants the other character to say or do, then commit as if your life depended on it.

TOM: Exactly. It's really hard to get distracted when there is such a tangible task at hand.

BRENT: It's also an effective memory device. Your drive and your partner's resistance spark the action and move it forward; you set each other up for the next line. That kind of tussling is very much alive in Mamet, and *Straight* has a similar dynamic. Still, it's possible that you may blank on your lines. What do you do when that happens?

TOM: No matter what, there are definitely moments where anyone would just space out on stage. Once you come out of that moment, it's important to just throw yourself back into the analysis and action that Practical Aesthetics dictates. Because we have such firm foundation, it's pretty easy to find your way back into the scene after you've "left it" for a little bit.

BRENT: And you have other characters to prompt you and help you find your way. Well, this has been a real pleasure. No doubt you have many great roles ahead of you. Thank you for talking with me.

TOM: Thanks, Brent!

24.

LINCOLN STOLLER ON THE SCIENCE AND METAPHYSICS OF MEMORY IN THE BODY

October 2016

A scientist and hypnotherapist takes the concept of muscle memory to new levels.

Lincoln Stoller's expertise spans the physical and metaphysical worlds. He earned a Ph.D. in quantum physics, ventured into neuroscience and psychology, and plunged into the realm of consciousness with training in hypnotherapy. His current enterprise is called **Mind Strength Balance** and focuses on issues of thought, growth, and identity. Lincoln works with individuals to hone their skills in problem solving, recognition, motor coordination, short term memory, and artistic expression, with the broader goal of helping them develop positive habits, strengthen relationships, enlarge their focus, heighten their awareness, and open their creative mind.

Although Lincoln does not work in the performing arts, his revelations about how memories can be stored in different parts of the body and how they manifest themselves physically are useful for those seeking to deepen their self-exploration.

BRENT: You've told me that You believe that people store relevant memories in different parts of their bodies. Can you elaborate on that for my readers?

LINCOLN: I think different parts of our body have their own personality and memory. Memory *works* when the attitudes and objectives of these parts are in harmony, and it fails when there is discord. You struggle to recall when the context is not relevant or agreeable, and recall assembles itself when you free-associate.

BRENT: So how, specifically?

LINCOLN: The association with our parts is reasonable: hands being involved in manipulation, and ankles with orientation. But it can be unusual, such as one's hands being involved with deceit for those of us who spent our youth shoplifting. The thoughts in our tissues reflect the emotions that were at play at the time. So, for the shoplifter operating from frustration, their hands may now carry these overtones. What deeper associations emerge when we wring our hands? Ask yourself, what feelings are in your hands?

BRENT: That's really fascinating! Actors tell me that part of getting into character means exploring with hyperawareness the physicality of their character—as well as the mental and emotional states that manifest themselves physically.

LINCOLN: I'm looking beyond the obvious and focusing on a dialog with organs, joints, and tissues. Speak to your gall bladder, converse with your uterus, respect the voice in your testicles. Imagine the stories of your body and develop them as separate identities. It's okay that you are making this up; that's how you conjure things into reality.

BRENT: Absolutely! Paying attention to these sensations, and where they reside, creates opportunities for reflection and self-knowledge.

LINCOLN: Consider a list of phone calls. For each call, associate the feeling it will evoke. Where in your body will each feeling reside? Connect those feelings with the calls and determine if the list of feelings is coherent or disparate. You might see this as a somato-emotional prescription for building the memory palace, but it's more than that. Each memory will have a correct place, not just a convenient one. You will better remember—and probably function better, too—if the feelings associated with the memories are coherent.

BRENT: You bring to mind some of the exercises that Stanislavski advocates in his method acting approach. An actor is asked to stand up, walk across the room, and close the door. The body language associated with these actions can take radically different forms, depending on the scene. How does the actor move if the reason for closing the door is to shut out a strong, cold wind blowing in from the outside? What if it's to stop listening to an annoying person in the next room? These physical forms of expression will come from different parts of the actor's body, even though the stimuli are imaginary.

LINCOLN: Return to the practical issue of storing memory in your body. If remembering is keeping things in mind, and not forgetting is retrieving things from memory, then remembering and not forgetting are different. Remembering is a process of making familiar, while not forgetting can be accomplished through habit. Such a habit is not the *things* to remember but rather a *means* of remembering them.

BRENT: This makes me think of the origin of writing systems that replaced the oral tradition. There's an oft-quoted passage in Plato's *Phaedrus* in which a speaker laments the invention of writing, what he terms a system of "reminding," which is inferior to "remembering." He claims that writing will discourage people from developing their memories and induce forgetfulness.

LINCOLN: We write checklists, develop routines, and become vigilant to changes in our environment. We behave differently when challenged, such as changing our gait when walking over rough terrain or becoming attentive when walking down stairs. We use sensations and body movement as a memory aid. Many of these triggers are unconscious, so it would stand to reason that by paying greater attention to these habits, we could improve our ability to record and recall.

BRENT: We agree on that. I firmly believe that awareness of one's physical movements, including writing in longhand, are strong aids to memory— muscle memory, in fact.

LINCOLN: Muscle memory is linked to a movement or sense, things that remind us to pay attention. We can intentionally imprint patterns through sense and movement for the purpose of remembering. We can heighten our awareness of movement and sensation using focus, visualization, and repetition. Regain sensation and we regain memory.

BRENT: Lincoln, you've given us so much food for thought, and we haven't even gotten to your hypnotic regression work! I want to make sure we cover that. Before we do, do you have anything you'd like to add about your perception of memory?

LINCOLN: Memory is not data. It is a process, and as a process it develops according to the needs of the organism. What we call a memory is a tapestry of associations, each being a one-dimensional thing without context, a rudimentary thing. Only when these threads of sequence, feeling, vision, name, emotion, sound, and story are woven together do we recognize the result as "a memory."

BRENT: And that story may be part fact and part fiction, correct? Our memories can play tricks on us over time. Age, experience, and other variables can color, cloud, and filter our recollections.

LINCOLN: It is important to acknowledge that no matter how certain our memory, it may be false. There is nothing wrong with this so long as you understand that memory serves a function and should be measured by its effect. Most of what we remember never happened, we just "copy and paste" to fill in between the things that did.

BRENT: That's a great segue to my last question. How does your work heighten people's self-awareness and ability to remember more going forward?

LINCOLN: I work with my clients' subjective measures of memory. I try to reframe a person's ideas in order to better fit these memories to the designs they are trying to create. The art is in the listening because neither their reality nor what they're trying to create is fully known to them, or to me.

BRENT: So, in essence, you listen less to what they say and more to what they mean.

LINCOLN: I try not to pay too much attention to their words, but rather to their lilt, rhythm, and melody, to hear what they're saying as a piece of music. I don't hang on every note but pay attention to the feelings and associations that are emerging in them and in me. I'm looking for a reality that's different from what they say, which means different from what they remember. I want to dis-understand my client's version, and re-understand their problem as an opportunity in the context of their history, circumstance, and abilities.

BRENT: You accomplish this by taking people into a trance, right?

LINCOLN: Yes. In trance, everything is more fluid, and suggestions trigger new associations which, in turn, create new memories. People say to me, "I don't know if I'm just making this up!" And I say, "It doesn't matter. You can't make up how you feel about it, and the feelings drive you."

BRENT: You've told me that what a person feels, regardless of the story, often becomes as powerful as an absolute certainty. It becomes, in effect, the truth. Their truth.

LINCOLN: Truth does not exist by itself. Truth is how you feel about something: the stove burns, sorrow motivates, love is meaningful. These truths hold beyond the reasons and memories on which they're built.

BRENT: So, you're not really sharpening their memory as much as you are helping them understand how they intrinsically remember—and feel— about an experience.

LINCOLN: The question is not how to improve your memory, but how to distill it. How to transfer the essential juice into your personality and, having done that, open yourself to receive new recollections of the past, and new memories moving into the future.

BRENT: And you believe that these memories that we carry forward actually have deeper roots in the past than we might imagine. Is that correct?

LINCOLN: We carry memories of our parents, and these are not memories of just our parents but our parents' memories of their parents as well. I always assume that it goes way back. We are working on growing out of our need to be parented, which is also our parents' need to be parented. We are growing into our ability to be parents... to our children, to our own parents, and to ourselves.

BRENT: What are the most useful, meaningful memories that we should strive to elicit?

LINCOLN: I see it as a process of rearranging our memories, like some great game of Tetris, where the pieces that fit together to "explain" each other then disappear. In the end, if we're lucky, the only memories we retain are the memories that define who we want to be. It is safe to say these are memories of love.

BRENT: Well, that is a beautiful sentiment to end on, Lincoln. Thank you so much for sharing your wisdom.

LINCOLN: It's been a pleasure.

25.

JASON BUTLER HARNER RECOMMENDS ALLITERATION FOR THE POST-40-YEAR-OLD BRAIN

March 2016

The Broadway actor reflects on pattern finding and the dangers of Shakespeare in excess.

Broadway actor Jason Butler Harner is no stranger to long, dense dialogue—from Tom Stoppard's epic *The Coast of Utopia* to the current production of Arthur Miller's *The Crucible,* in which he plays the fearsome Reverend Samuel Parris. We spoke after a preview performance of the latter at the Walter Kerr Theatre.

BRENT: How did you memorize your lines for this role?

JASON: From the first rehearsal we had to be off book. That's pretty demanding. As for memorization techniques, I have many. These days I focus a lot on alliteration.

BRENT: By repeating the phrases out loud?

JASON: I write out the first letter of every word and all punctuation. The punctuation is very important; it provides structure.

BRENT: Give me an example.

JASON: One of my lines is "Out of here—out of my sight!" That works out to O O H — O O M S !

BRENT: What fascinating shorthand! Have you always done this?

JASON: As I get older, past 40, memorization gets harder. In college, I could flip through all my lines while walking from home to class.

BRENT: But then, you were 19.

JASON: Don't remind me!

BRENT: What about associating your lines with physical markers on stage?

JASON: Nah, I don't do that. I've tried, but it just makes me aware that I'm acting. I get too self-conscious, too into my own head.

BRENT: That's unusual. You must have other anchors.

JASON: Well, you certainly hear more the more you do a play. And you become aware of echoes, the repetition of patterns.

BRENT: Like your alliteration approach.

JASON: Right, they form a sort of rhythm. It's fun to echo the words. My character, Rev. Parris, says a lot of "surely" and "some." Throughout the play, words ricochet among the characters. You hear a lot of "black" and "white"—"blacken my face," "whiten my name," for example.

BRENT: Interesting. It's almost like freestyle Shakespearean meter.

JASON: The language is more contemporary, not archaic.

BRENT: Where did you study acting?

JASON: VCU, Virginia Commonwealth University in Richmond. Since you mention Shakespeare, I'll tell you a funny story. I had a teacher named Janet Rodgers who lived and breathed Shakespeare. One morning she woke up and could speak only in iambic pentameter. She had to go to a doctor to snap out of it. It's true; you can look it up!

BRENT: I believe you! Last question, what's the best advice you've ever gotten about how to learn your lines?

JASON: Great way to end! There's a wonderful video interview with Peter O'Toole that I saw on Facebook. He says, "The old-fashioned word for it was study. You go alone; you have no observer, no interlocutor. An unobserved, uninhibited private study is the backbone of any fine actor or actress."

BRENT: Thank you, Jason. You radiate such fierce intensity on stage, but you're really easygoing in person.

JASON: Thank you for taking an interest in what I do and seeing the play.

THE PLAYWRIGHT'S
PERSPECTIVE

26.
___

RINNE GROFF'S APPROACH TO WRITING MEMORABLE (AND AWARD-WINNING) PLAYS

October 2016

A New York playwright explores a "build in intensity" as a way to master a text.

Playwright and performer Rinne Groff was trained at Yale University and New York University's Tisch School of the Arts, where she currently teaches. A founding member of Elevator Repair Service Theater Company, she has been a part of the writing, staging, and performing of their shows since the company's inception in 1991. Groff has received a Guggenheim Award and Whiting Award for Drama, as well as a fellowship from the MacDowell Colony.

BRENT: When you write a play, how much do you think about how the actors will approach memorizing the text?

RINNE: I don't think about it too much. In general, I find actors to be amazingly adept at memorizing text. It's one of the muscles which actors, especially theater actors, have developed mightily. I recently wrote a play with a ten-minute monologue at the center. I worried about the actor's ability to learn it. To my amazement, not only did she learn it, but during previews, when we were still making changes to the script, she could take in a re-written line in the afternoon and deliver it on stage flawlessly in performance that night. That's an actor with a gift for text.

BRENT: That is indeed a talent! Who is she?

RINNE: Her name is Bree Elrod.

BRENT: Thank you. I will look her up. Do you think your structure, word choice, blocking, etc. facilitate the learning of the text by the actors?

RINNE: I don't structure text to make it easier to learn, but when an actor struggles with a section or repeatedly gets something wrong in rehearsal, I make an effort to explain my word choice and what I believe to be the intention behind a line. Generally, once the actor has that understanding (*why* this word and not that word, or how this topic *leads* to that topic in the character's mind), the mistake corrects itself.

BRENT: Interesting. Have you ever met a writer who intentionally put memory aids into the text?

RINNE: When working on a musical with a quite experienced lyric writer, he shared with me what he does with a string of words that could potentially go in any order. Example: in the first chorus they sing, "I love you deeply," the second time, "I love you madly," and the third, "I love you truly." Then he puts those differentiated words in alphabetical order so that it aids in the memorization. Thus, deeply, madly, truly.

BRENT: I get the impression that you would take a different tack.

RINNE: I think I'd approach the same problem more in terms of the build: Which is the least intense? Probably "deeply." Then we could discuss if "madly" or "truly" were the most extreme expression of love from this character because with lists in drama, one always wants them to build in intensity. So again, I suppose I'm confessing to the internal logic system of memorization—finding the key that unlocks the reason for a particular structure or word choice—rather than the strictly mnemonic.

BRENT: Have you ever made changes to a script because it was too difficult to memorize?

RINNE: Not exactly. But if an actor struggles mightily with a section of text, it's either because there's something he doesn't understand, or there's something I don't understand. If an actor can point out to me what it is that I'm missing that makes it difficult for him to keep ahold of the text (and if I think he's correct in his assessment), I will joyously change the line to one that makes more sense and, thus, is easier to remember.

BRENT: What methods do you use to memorize scripts or other material for public presentation?

RINNE: As I suppose you can gather from my previous answers, understanding is key: why this word, why this structure, why this apparent veer to a new topic. If I understand the psychology, then the progression of words follows naturally. If I am struggling with a line, I try to come up with an ironclad reason why it has to be the way it is and no other way, and that reasoning will flash before my eyes, so to speak, as I get to the particular tricky section.

BRENT: How do you prepare physically for a presentation?

RINNE: The more pedestrian answer is: I read it out loud, again, and again, and again. I look at it, put down the book, say it out loud, check that I got it right, and repeat. In short, I practice. Like most things, learning a speech requires practice.

BRENT: I read a terrific quote recently in a book about Stanislavski's method acting approach. To paraphrase, a patient doesn't get better by reading the prescription; he must take the medicine. I remind students in my workshop that memorization is akin to learning a foreign language: you have to *actively* write, read, speak, and hear the text in order to internalize it. Last question: any plans for you to take the stage again?

RINNE: I'm performing on stage for the first time in 14 years come next fall, and I've been in some workshops leading up to it. I was never the best memorizer, one of those people to whom it seems to come effortlessly, but I find that now, being out of practice, I definitely have to work a little harder to get the words into my head. But they do come!

BRENT: You're taking it on the right way. It will be like getting back on a bicycle.

RINNE: Thank you. I hope these answers are useful.

BRENT: They absolutely are. You have been very generous with your time and beautifully articulated insights. Thank you!

27.

BEN BONNEMA ON WRITING LYRICS THAT STICK

August 2017

A musical theater composer sees a correlation between structure and intuition.

Ben Bonnema is a composer-lyricist and recipient of a 2017 Jonathan Larson Grant by the American Theatre Wing. One of Ben's claims to fame is his having written the book, music, and lyrics to Adult Swim's *Peter Panic*, a musical video game that's been played by over a half million people. His musical theater credits are numerous and include sound design and composition for the award-winning *Sleep No More*, as well as orchestrations for Ana Gasteyer's album "I'm Hip." We met at an event sponsored by the Rhinebeck Writers Retreat, a non-profit that provides weeklong residencies to musical theater writers to develop their shows.

BRENT: When you write a show, how much do you think about how the actors will learn the text?

BEN: My focus when writing tends to be less on how the actor will memorize and more on if the text feels natural and authentic. I believe that if the actor is fully embodying the character and the text flows in a way that's character-based, it'll make it easier to memorize.

BRENT: Very thoughtful. You also write songs, which do not sound like natural speech. What is your approach there?

BEN: When writing songs, I think that form and structure make all the difference in memorization. If I write with a clear form that still manages to throw in some surprises, I'd hope the process of learning the text is simpler.

BRENT: What do you think makes musicals such a powerful medium to capture emotionally charged themes?

BEN: I can remember melodies much easier than lyrics, and I think there's an evolutionary reason for that. A while ago I read *This Is Your Brain On Music* by Daniel Levitin, and it talked about how inherently connected music is with emotion. Our brain hears music like it does emotion in human voices.

BRENT: Interesting. What example comes to mind?

BEN: For example, a high violin line that glisses down may unconsciously remind our brains of someone crying. We evolved to discern people's emotional states, and so our brain hears music that way—it's almost an accident of evolution. I love this idea, and it's fun to think about while writing.

BRENT: I will look for Levitin's book. Oliver Sacks' work, *Musicophilia,* also explores the unique impact of music on our brains; there are places that music can take us that ordinary speech does not. Beyond the "memorability" of music, how else do you structure your work to facilitate the actors' learning of the text?

BEN: I can't speak for the more directorial aspects, like blocking, but structure is huge. Take the AABA form. If you've set up a specific rhyme scheme in the first A, the actor can reasonably expect for the same rhyme scheme in the second and final A sections. The details will be different, but you know as an actor that you have the structure to fall back on.

BRENT: Right, some actors and playwrights have told me that they are often on the lookout for linguistic triggers, like rhyme, meter, or homophones. Shakespearean scholar Daniel Spector told me in an interview about how the iambic pentameter and rhyme scheme helped the audience remember the dialogue almost as well as the actors.

BEN: Consistency of scansion [the rhythm of a line of verse] seems to be a huge help in facilitating the learning of the text.

BRENT: Have you ever made changes to a script because an actor found something too difficult to memorize?

BEN: I think it's important to pay attention to the actor's instincts. If they're saying the wrong word repeatedly in rehearsal, I might evaluate if their choice is more natural or makes more sense. I know for sure I've done this with melodies. Like, "Oh yeah, what you're singing does make more sense with the chord, let's go with that." I've never thought of it strictly in terms of memorization, but I would guess that it's easier to memorize what feels natural, both text and music.

BRENT: When there is repetition of certain phrases or melodies, do you (or the actors) ever get confused about what particular line comes next?

BEN: I think that can definitely be the case, and what can help is making sure that the repeated section has a different emotional state. Confusion comes when the phrases are almost interchangeable. But if the second verse with the exact same rhyme scheme is more emotionally charged than the first, that seems to help.

BRENT: Excellent point. Does a particular verse spring to mind?

BEN: Martin Dickinson—one of the actors in our show *One Way* at the Page to Stage Festival in London—said, "The reason that you repeat a phrase is because the intention has grown. The action comes from the line after the repeated lyric. If you can link the action to the feeling, then you won't forget. There are only two reasons that actors forget lines— one, you don't know the lines properly. Two, you're not concentrating." I think that was a Laurence Olivier quote.

BRENT: Tell me about other contexts in which you have used memorization techniques.

BEN: We're often in situations where we get a new cast and have to quickly memorize everyone's names. I'll try a few things—I might visualize the person's face and repeat their name in my head; I might see what in that person reminds me of someone else I know with the same name; I might stare at the casting sheet with names and photos for a solid ten minutes. Just depends.

BRENT: You are a keen observer. In your case, the actors who make the final cut must have made a deeper impression on you, so you're more attentive to their face, body language, and emotional range.

BEN: It helps when you've been through the whole audition and casting process for the show—even though you've seen a million people, there was something about their performance during the audition that stuck out (probably because it made you feel things), and so it can be easy to think, "Ah yes, that's Karen, who sang 'Losing My Mind' and made me cry."

BRENT: Thanks so much for your time and wisdom, Ben. It's greatly appreciated. Best wishes for success with *One Way*.

BEN: Thank you!

28.

PETER ALEXANDER ON THE PERSISTENCE OF MUSICAL MEMORY

June 2016

Acomposer for musical theater reveals what makes melodies and lyrics stick.

San Francisco Bay Area–based composer Peter Alexander is a proud member of the Dramatists Guild of America and graduate of the Academy for New Musical Theater.

Peter's compositions reference styles ranging from J.S. Bach to Jason Robert Brown. His lyric writing pays tribute to such luminaries as Stephen Sondheim and Joni Mitchell. Peter was the composer and co-lyricist for *Can't Say I Do*, a musical romp through the subjects of family and gay marriage, and he recently wrote book, lyrics, and music for *In the Hands of the Raven*, a love-story musical about grief, guiding forces, and letting go. We are old friends from my years living in California.

BRENT: When you write the book, lyrics, and music for a work like *In the Hands of the Raven*, do you think about how the performers will commit their parts to memory?

PETER: The short simple answer is just, no. I never think about memorization when I'm *writing*. It's when I'm editing that memorization even enters my thoughts, and even then it's not until I'm editing during the process of working with actors and singers.

BRENT: Interesting. What happens next?

PETER: When a theatre piece gets to the workshopping stage, or when I'm asking a singer to learn a song for me, then I really pay attention to the places where they stumble, get tongue tied, or have any kind of trouble. This points at the problems in the writing.

BRENT: That speaks well of you, that you're open to change. Any other occasions where this is the case?

PETER: This also holds for when I'm trying to learn something, or for example, when I'm trying to make a demo recording. If I have trouble learning something, I generally know that it's not right yet. If I see or hear an actor struggling with a certain passage repeatedly, I always ask myself, "Is the difficulty in the passage?" The difficulty is usually not with the actor.

BRENT: You've written emotionally charged shows about social issues, like *Can't Say I Do*, which called for legalizing same-sex marriage. What do you think makes musicals an especially powerful medium to memorialize experiences?

PETER: Musicals (and really all theater for that matter) have to be about personally charged issues. If they weren't, we wouldn't want to watch them. Someone famous once said, "When words fail, characters sing. When singing isn't enough, we make them dance. When dancing isn't enough, we make them do all three at the same time. That's how you get musicals."

BRENT: That's brilliant. Any idea what the origin is?

PETER: Sorry, but I have no idea who said this, and I'm sure that my quotation is not very accurate. Nonetheless, people connect to music on a visceral level. It engages something in us, reactions that frequently we are not even aware of.

BRENT: Sounds like you have some specific instances in mind.

PETER: I'm reminded of an experience I had shortly after seeing the movie *Arachnophobia,* which uses parts of the Berlioz *Symphonie Fantastique* in the score. A roommate who had seen the movie with me stepped into my room to visit while I was listening to the Berlioz sometime during the week after we had seen the movie. A few minutes after coming in, she left, and the next day she told me that she felt all creepy all of the sudden but had no idea why. I thought immediately that she had been taken back into the movie by the music.

BRENT: Music can be transporting that way.

PETER: Similarly, there's an old Noel Coward directed film, *Brief Encounter,* which uses the Rachmaninoff Second Piano Concerto as underscore throughout the movie. Whenever I listen to that piece of music now, it takes me through the emotional journey I experienced the first time I saw the movie. By today's standards, the movie feels pretty overdone, but when I first saw it, I went right along for the ride.

BRENT: I know what you mean. I've seen the stage version of *Brief Encounter* and recall it viscerally. In fact, there's a fascinating reversal at one point. A character experiences a profound romantic loss, and the Rachmaninoff swells up dramatically, off-stage. The music continues playing into the next scene, but it's no longer mood music; it's coming from a blaring radio on stage.

PETER: Yes! Every time I hear that concerto, I go on the same emotional journey from the combination of the film and the music.

BRENT: How do you perceive the flow of your own compositions? Do you think of the notes progressing in linear fashion like the plot of a story?

PETER: This feels like a very odd question for me. I don't think I'm really able to perceive the flow of my own music. I'm too close to it. For me, one of the advantages of being the composer is that I don't have to memorize my own work. Generally, I find it much more difficult to memorize my own work than that of others. I've always told myself that it's because my own work changes so much while I'm writing it. I'm a very fussy lyricist. I change things a lot. I have also written many songs, which have several different versions.

BRENT: Give me an example.

PETER: "Here With Me" is one of the songs from *In the Hands of the Raven* which begins, "Here it is again, June 17th, another candle on your cake." This is a re-lyric of a personal song I wrote which begins, "I still imagine ev'ry August 4th, another candle on your cake." When I'm writing them, my songs are like jigsaw puzzles. Sometimes a chorus idea that I jotted down three months ago goes with the verse I just heard this morning. My writing process is not very linear at all. Again, linear comes into play when I'm editing, which I told you about earlier.

BRENT: Do you ever associate visuals with music or lyrics to remember them?

PETER: As to visuals, yes, I'm a very visual person. As I'm writing, I visualize stage sets, even actors' blocking. Frequently, it's very cinematic in my head, but that's just what keeps the characters real in my head while I'm writing. I don't really use it consciously to help me with memorization. Maybe if I did, I'd be better at memorization!

BRENT: When there is repetition of certain phrases or melodies, do you ever get confused about what particular line comes next?

PETER: Of course. The first thing that comes to mind is Sondheim's "Being Alive" from *Company:*

> Somebody hold me too close.
> Somebody hurt me too deep.
> Somebody sit in my chair,
> And ruin my sleep,
> And make me aware,

Of being alive.

Being alive.

The rhyme, the structure, and the alliteration all help me with memorization, but it's a sort of mental pathway of ideas that I have to find for myself that really gets me through the whole song. Like this: "hold me too close" (what will that do?), "hurt me too deep" (how do you do that?), you "sit in my chair," then you "ruin my sleep," which all "makes me aware of being alive."

The next verse begins, "Somebody need me too much." And the final verse with "Somebody crowd me with love." And if I sing "need" when I'm supposed to sing "hold," then I'm going to sing the rest of the verse that goes with "need." Sometimes it feels like a giant game of Russian roulette inside my brain. And I just get to follow it around in circles.

BRENT: You're not alone. It can be easy to take the wrong fork in the road. Some of the ways to make lyrics stick are either to visualize the progression in some crazy over-the-top way or make up an acrostic that uses the first letter of the primary changed words.

PETER: I'll have to give that a try!

BRENT: Do you have any theories about the relationship between music and memory?

PETER: The relationship between music and memory is something I marvel at more than I think I understand or can explain. One of my grandmothers had water on the brain, which presented a lot like Alzheimer's. I often wonder what it was like for her. But what I can't forget is one time when she was in my car for about an hour at Christmas time, and I had a CD of Christmas music playing in the car. She knew every word to every Christmas carol, including "O Tannenbaum" in German. During the five seconds between each song, she was almost frantic about what was coming next, but the minute a song started, she was singing, she was in it. She wasn't thinking about what came next, she just kept singing.

BRENT: The long-term memories were more deeply rooted in her mind; that's pretty common. It was the uncertainty of the silence and its unknown duration that caused her to panic.

PETER: That's a good point. In my own personal experience, the biggest barrier to memory is fear and panic. When I get worried about what my next line is, or when I'm thinking, "Will I remember the next lyric?" That's when I forget. For me, there's a certain amount of letting go that helps me remember. I have to study the lines or lyrics. I have to know that I have rehearsed properly. But in performance, mostly I have to trust that they will be there. And when I do (trust), they are (there).

BRENT: Thank you so much, Peter. You are gifted with sensitivity and creativity.

PETER: I may have gone off topic a bit, but this was fun!

BLANKING AND GETTING
BACK ON TRACK

29.

A PRIVATE MASTER CLASS
WITH MICHAEL RHODES
October 2015

A New York actor provides invaluable tips for anyone who speaks publicly.

Stage actor Michael Rhodes is also the artistic director of the Tangent Theatre Company in Tivoli, NY. His impressive list of regional theater credits runs the gamut from Shakespeare to Albee to Beckett. Here, he offers deep, practical insights into memorization, character, overcoming forgotten lines, the power of breathing, and what to do with your hands while giving a speech.

BRENT: How do you approach memorizing lengthy dialogue?

MICHAEL: The easiest way for me to memorize longer passages is by determining the logic of why these particular words are being said. It's primarily analyzing speech patterns as well as thought patterns; what key words, thoughts, or actions in the text lead into the following sentence? Sometimes, it's not easy.

BRENT: In what play did you find this difficult?

MICHAEL: When I did *The Zoo Story,* my character had a complex 20-plus-minute monologue. It was extremely difficult for me at the time and left me raging as I tried to learn it because there didn't seem to be a logic to some of the jumps in the character's thought pattern. But once I stopped trying to just learn the words and instead began to chart not just "what" was being said, but also my interpretation of "why" my character was saying this—and making decisions on what specific word in the text connected to the following character thought—the entire monologue began to make sense and opened a door to Edward Albee's amazing command of language. I can probably still recite it all to this day.

BRENT: Does being an actor make it easy for you to do public speaking as Tangent Theatre Company's Artistic Director?

MICHAEL: I'm a pretty big introvert, which may be ironic for an actor, and when I have someone else's lines to say, pretending to be someone else, I'm okay in front of a crowd because I have something so specific—words and actions—to concentrate on during the play. But as Artistic Director of Tangent, I often have to be "myself" and speak in front of groups and audiences. There is always that panic of "what am I talking about?" before going in front of the crowd. But I take a breath and let it out (the exhalation is important to release tension) and then ask myself, "Why am I talking?" That's an easier answer because I'm reminded why I'm there, and that informs the "what."

BRENT: How have you or another actor recovered when your mind has gone blank on stage?

MICHAEL: I think every actor has more of these than they'd like to admit. Going up on a line is inevitable. The tiniest thing can distract and suddenly you're adrift. The language in the play *Doubt,* Tangent's first production in Tivoli, is so lean and tightly constructed to drive the play forward, that even a single skipped word could derail us and we'd be lost.

BRENT: What you're saying holds particularly true for Shakespeare.

MICHAEL: I remember a production of *The Tempest* many years ago and I was playing Prospero. I was in the middle of a scene with the actress playing my daughter. I'm delivering a certain passage of lines (I clearly remember her back was to me and we were downstage facing the audience), the words were flowing and, in my mind, I suddenly see a road sign in the distance. Still speaking—it was a long, Shakespearean passage—I could see that the approaching mental road sign read: "You Don't Know Any Lines Past This Point."

BRENT: Yikes! What did that feel like?

MICHAEL: Terror, of course. But I kept going. Just as I was about to pass the imaginary sign, there was a word—and I can't remember the word, unfortunately, as this was over 20 years ago now—that sparked the "why" that led to the next sentence, and I made it through the rest of the passage.

BRENT: Any advice for what anyone should do in that situation?

MICHAEL: Any actor will tell you that when you go up on a line in a scene, breathe. Take that moment (and that second or two feels like an ungodly 15 minutes of dead silence on stage), look at your scene partner, take a breath, think about the circumstance of the scene, and usually the line comes back to you.

BRENT: In what show did this practice work for you?

MICHAEL: An early Tangent production in New York City was *Waiting for Godot*. The actor I was playing Estragon to his Vladimir skipped a page or two of the script, he realized, and blanked. He tried a line but it was too far ahead in the script to pick up. Then he tried to back up and find the line he jumped. To each of these I could only give a tiny shake of my head. Ordinarily, when your partner doesn't know where they are, you try and feed them a clue but you just can't improvise Beckett and I could only watch helplessly. Eyes wide and locked on each other, he took that moment, took a breath, and gingerly tried a line, and he started to find his footing and we were back on track.

BRENT: Your experience speaks to the value of knowing the other characters' lines as well as your own so that you know your cues. On stage you are each other's safety nets.

MICHAEL: He and I still say it is the most present we have ever been in a moment on stage.

BRENT: I want to ask you about using your imagination to get into character.

MICHAEL: I always use my imagination. I have to put myself into those characters' shoes (literally: the shoes are always an early key for me), think about those circumstances the character is going through and, first, find any personal similarities to past experiences. Then I imagine not just myself in that situation but start building from there, imagining a reality of those circumstances, and that provides a great key for me to play a character, both internally and with my scene partner(s), which hopefully sparks some life into the dynamics of the play.

BRENT: What are some actions that you've taken to make those fictional experiences more vivid?

MICHAEL: I can try many things to find keys to open all those internal doors looking for my click for the character. I've gone to museums to try and find a painting that I felt expressed my character; not so much a literal interpretation of the character, but something that I could feel that captured the essence of who I was playing (Pollock for *The Zoo Story*, the dogs playing poker for *American Buffalo*). I've written histories for my characters; we would improvise situations between characters from before the events of the play or events between scenes of the play, music to bring yourself to an emotional place, just many, many things.

BRENT: Writing histories is an effective method. I heard the novelist Gillian Flynn say that to develop the twisted psyche of Amy Dunne in *Gone Girl,* she wrote essays that the character might have composed as a high school student.

MICHAEL: Francis Ford Coppola would tell his actors, "Do as much preparation as you want, but when it's time to do it, forget it all." Why? Because the preparation has created the foundation you need, and there's no need to force what you're already carrying. The text and your fellow actors should take it from there.

BRENT: The last area I want to explore with you is physicality. How does that inform memorization?

MICHAEL: I recently read a great interview with an acting teacher who posits that any character's motivation/action comes from one of three places: the head, the heart, or below the belt. That informs with great simplicity where your character leads from and, suddenly, I know how to stand, walk, where the voice comes from and that, in turn, helps form and inform the inner life of a character. It's great to keep things that simple, so that you're not carrying a ton of things in your head onstage—lines, intention, posture, etc.—which leaves you open.

BRENT: You have the best advice I've ever heard about what people in a public speaking role should do with their hands.

MICHAEL: Hands are the worst. What do you do with these things? I think hands flapping about onstage usually mean an actor isn't comfortable with their lines yet. I had an actor friend who was also a teacher, and I remember a trick he told a young actor who looked like his hands were conducting a symphony during a rehearsal: just press your thumb lightly against your middle finger. The audience can't see it, and it's a simple, non-intrusive action that takes the worry of what to do with those hands away. Your hands almost instinctively drop to your sides. Suddenly, they only move when you want them to.

BRENT: That's brilliant.

BRENT: A recurring theme in these interviews is that mistakes can be gifts. How has this played out in your acting?

MICHAEL: In rehearsals, some of those things work, most do not—and that's the way it should be. I always say that rehearsals are our chance to get it wrong, to get the bad choices out of the way, which eventually clears the path; I start to find my way and settle in. But sometimes the path is rocky, and that's okay. Any little techniques are designed to help us through the parts we can't easily reach.

BRENT: I feel like I've just finished a Master Class! I can't thank you enough for all your insights and ideas.

MICHAEL: You are welcome. See you at the theater!

30.

GREG SKURA AND THE MAGICAL POWER OF CURIOSITY

February 2018

A New York–based actor and executive coach offers a surefire way to banish anxiety both on stage and off.

Greg Skura's work as an actor and director has been seen across a variety of media, including theater, television, film, interactive games, and radio. He apprenticed with The Dorset Theatre Festival and at The Jupiter Theatre before moving to New York City to embark on a career as a professional actor. While there, Greg had the great fortune of assisting and learning from legendary theater artist Joseph Chaikin, who deepened his knowledge of acting and directing and transformed his ideas around presence, on stage and in life. Greg has also worked for the last decade as a leadership coach and communications consultant.

BRENT: Tell me, what's the most challenging role you've ever had to prepare for in terms of memorization?

GREG: It's good timing to get that question now, theoretically and practically. I have a monster of a part to learn for a play called *There Is a Happiness That Morning Is* by Mickle Maher. I just got cast. In the sixty-page script, 50 pages of the lines are in verse, rhyming couplets, actually. The play explores themes in the poetry of William Blake.

BRENT: Cool! When and where does the play run?

GREG: It opens this September at the Bridge Street Theatre in Catskill, New York.

BRENT: And how will you tackle this "monster of a part"?

GREG: This won't be a very sexy answer, but I learn my lines mostly by rote. I break down the lines into beats.

BRENT: And do you define beats as a word? A phrase? A section?

GREG: Any and all. A beat is a shift in both *attention* and *intention*. It's a momentary pause that relates to a change or decision.

BRENT: So, whatever moves the action forward.

GREG: Exactly. With a ruler and a pencil, I mark out the beats on the page. They may change over the course of rehearsals. I bring my instincts and see how they evolve. For example, I may have a sentence like, "I got in the car to go to the store to buy bread." I then ask myself, what kind of vehicle did I get into—my truck? No, my car. To go where? To the store. To buy what? A loaf of bread.

BRENT: This must help you more deeply understand the character's function and motivation.

GREG: It does. A teacher of mine used to liken it to stringing pearls. Or putting beads on a bracelet. Each bead represents a beat.

BRENT: Do you ever use any visualization or association techniques?

GREG: If I have a list of items, I'll make an acrostic. If I were going to the store to buy marbles, apples, cookies, and a knife, I'd think of the word MACK to remind me of the first letter of each item. Beyond that, I can't say I have a formal system. I repeat my lines over and over again. It's sort of like ironing.

BRENT: Is there anything special you do when you run lines with your scene partner?

GREG: You want to run lines as fast as you can. It's your chance to get your mouth around the words and know how they feel.

BRENT: Right, another actor, Carole Schweid, mentioned the benefits of a "speed-through rehearsal." If you can clearly articulate your lines at high speed, you have probably internalized them. This must be different than rehearsing for television.

GREG: In the film process, there's very little, if any, rehearsal—often just blocking for the cameras. You come in knowing your lines. Before that, you do your research and prep around the world of the film to bring the character to life. The theater process is a different animal.

BRENT: Has you mind ever gone blank on stage? If so, how did you recover?

GREG: In the interview you did with Michael Rhodes back in 2015, I was the one he mentioned who played Vladimir to his Estragon in *Waiting for Godot* down in New York City.

BRENT: I remember that! It was just the two of you on stage, and Michael kept waiting for you to deliver your line.

GREG: It was the most terrifying and the best experience I've ever had.

BRENT: I suppose it teaches you what you're capable of. How resilient you are.

GREG: And you realize the world doesn't end. What happened was, my mind went blank and then I made a crucial mistake: I visualized the physical script. That action took me out of the play and into my head. My impulse was to kind of hide. I turned upstage and had my back to the audience. Five or six seconds went by; it might as well have been an hour. You can't run off stage. I told myself, "Breathe, just breathe."

BRENT: What else was going through your mind?

GREG: An acting teacher once told us, "Look for your lines in the set. Trust that you'll find them there." The problem with *Godot* is that there really isn't much of a set, just a tree and a rock. There are no lines there. Fifteen seconds must have gone by. There was one more prop, though: a fedora, which belongs to another character named Lucky. And I remembered at that moment that I had a line referring to Lucky's hat. So I pointed and said the line "Lucky's hat!" The problem was that that line occurs three pages later in the play. But Michael stayed with me; he said the line that followed "Lucky's hat." We were enough in sync that we performed another three pages' worth of material, then jumped back six pages, filled in the three we had skipped, and then leapt forward to pick up after the three pages we had done out of order.

BRENT: That is a testament to excellent on-stage chemistry!

GREG: And it does make for a good story. The best advice I can offer anyone in this situation is to get curious.

BRENT: Say more.

GREG: Curiosity stops anxiety. Place the attention outside of yourself. It decreases the release of stress hormones associated with anxiety. It's impossible to be curious and anxious at the same time. That's what led me to look around the set for my lines.

BRENT: That is the best advice for anyone in any anxiety-producing situation! This may be a good time to ask about your executive coaching. How does your acting tie into that?

GREG: Coaching and acting feed each other. I practice something I call open-channel coaching. The goal is to let things flow and let go of judgment. Be open to exploring, not being told what to do. The idea is that we can choose our "performance" in any scene in our life, on stage or off. We must ask ourselves the question, "How do we choose to show up?"

BRENT: Being acutely aware of one's surroundings is something people don't do enough. When I worked at an improv theater company, we were always mindful about noticing more and reading the room—essentially, being present.

GREG: Exactly. What I do comes from a tradition of "presence-based" coaching. As humans, we want more of what feels good and less of what feels bad. If it feels good, we keep doing it. If it feels bad, we are tempted to avoid it, or to take a pill to make it go away. We don't listen enough to the internal and external signals to learn from them so that we can make a wise, productive change on our own.

BRENT: How does your presence-based coaching apply in a situation like helping someone prepare for a job interview?

GREG: People go into a job interview thinking, "Like me, like me, like me!" or "Hire me, hire me, hire me!" Is that really the best way to show up? I recommend making the choice to impress upon the interviewers that I'm here to build a relationship, one on one with each potential colleague. As an actor, I build that relationship with my fellow actors, and with an audience. Be curious. Prepare. Know who's in the audience and what the hot button issues are.

BRENT: Know those issues either to avoid them or prepare for them. For a communications job, I remember being encouraged to think of five questions you hope they don't ask you and have the answers ready—because those are the questions you will get. And it's okay to say you've considered the issue and don't have an answer—yet.

GREG: When you prepare for your interview, it's important to simplify, to distill key word phrases. Put them into buckets. And if you are doing a PowerPoint presentation, remember that bullet points are cue cards, not billboards.

BRENT: Right, it's counterproductive in PowerPoint when presenters throw dense blocks of text up on the screen. There should just be a few words to trigger and summarize the point.

GREG: And, again, you can use acrostics to remember your points so that you're looking at the audience, not at the screen.

BRENT: Anything else?

GREG: There's also the angle of a "growth" mindset vs. a "fixed" one. They've done experiments on this. If you tell a group of people that they're naturally smart and performed well on a task, they're unlikely to take on the challenge of going to the next level. If you tell them that it's obvious they put a lot of effort into succeeding, it motivates them to reach for more.

BRENT: That's an excellent recommendation for managers who want to keep their employees motivated. Well, thanks, Greg. You've made a compelling case for the value of the performing arts for personal and social transformation.

GREG: I credit one of my mentors, Joseph Chaikin, who directed the Open Theater in the 1960s and wrote the seminal book *The Presence of the Actor.* He focused on communal playmaking and the sound, movement, and form of others like Martha Graham. The positive effects on both self and the external world can't be overstated.

BRENT: I look forward to seeing you on stage in September for the Mickle Maher play in Catskill.

GREG: Thank you for your time! It's been great talking with you as well.

31

WHY JAMES GLEASON LIVES AND BREATHES HIS CHARACTER
June 2016

A Broadway actor discusses commitment and the importance of staying in character.

James Gleason is simply divine as the angel Gabriel in the hilarious Broadway production of *An Act of God*, starring Sean Hayes as The Almighty. The Los Angeles–based performer traces his thespian roots back to the Groundlings improv troupe. An actor, playwright, and voiceover artist, he boasts impressive credentials on stage and screen in comedy, dramas, and everything in between. We talked about the challenges of memorization and what to do when your mind goes blank on stage.

BRENT: What's the most challenging role you've ever prepared for in terms of memorization?

JAMES: I did a production of *The Weir* by Conor McPherson at the Geffen Playhouse in LA. I was the standby for John Mahoney [from the TV show "Frasier"] for the lead role of Jack. Since John was doing "Frasier" at the time, I was contracted to do the role when John was off filming. However, since John was the actor hired to play the role in the production, I received minimal rehearsal.

BRENT: That must have put you at a disadvantage.

JAMES: This is very difficult material with an Irish brogue, and you never leave the stage for the entire show. I have never worked harder in my life. I worked on my own every chance I got.

BRENT: You must have run lines with others, right?

JAMES: I was blessed to have a line coach named Louis Turenne who helped me. Louis volunteered his time and spent hours with me every day—explaining the dialogue, drilling the words to make sure they were exact, and being a wonderful moral support. Without his hard work, I'm not sure I could have done this role.

BRENT: So everything went swimmingly?

JAMES: Here's the rest of the story. I go on the last preview because John is working. We did a run-through in the afternoon, and I was letter perfect. That night I am on for the first time. We start, and for the first five minutes I am sailing along. I'm very confident. I remember turning up stage to look at something and saying to myself, "I know this material cold." I turned around, and I was completely up. No idea of the next line!

BRENT: Good God! What did you do next?

JAMES: I looked at the other actor in the play, he looks at me: nothing. I look at the audience: nothing. In my head it felt like three hours, but it was only maybe ten seconds. I finally just started talking. I made no sense in terms of the play, but I stayed in character, and then all that training and hard work paid off. The lines returned, and off we went.

BRENT: Ideally, you took a deep breath at some point during those harrowing moments. What did you learn from this experience?

JAMES: The lesson is: "Don't ever *assume* you know it."

BRENT: Some actors use visualization techniques to associate dialogue with a physical part of the stage. Do you ever do that?

JAMES: The beauty of rehearsal is that always gives you points of reference that help with lines and memorization. A glass may remind you of a speech about drinking or a chair of a long journey you were on and now you are happy to be home. Everything in the rehearsal process is part of learning a role.

BRENT: What's the best advice you can give performers who need to memorize their lines?

JAMES: Nothing replaces hard work. I know that sounds trite, but the more time you spend on a script, the more you will get out of it, and the more an audience will enjoy the performance. Know the material so you can do it in your sleep, and then work on it some more. The goal is to live as the character; the lines are only the facility to bring the character to the audience. This is what being a professional is all about.

BRENT: Thank you, James. It's been a thrill to talk with you. You've made me feel like I've been right alongside you on stage, during both your happiest and scariest moments.

JAMES: I am glad you are happy. Good luck with your book. I hope you sell a million!

PLAYING TOGETHER

32.

PATRICIA RYAN MADSON ON IMPROVISATION AND MENTAL AGILITY

September 2015

The author and Stanford professor drives home the therapeutic benefits of improvisation in interpersonal relationships.

Patricia Ryan Madson is the author of *Improv Wisdom: Don't Prepare, Just Show Up* and a Professor Emerita from Stanford University. She headed up the undergraduate acting and improvisation programs and founded the Creativity Initiative at Stanford. As a consultant, Patricia has introduced thousands of business leaders, wellness practitioners, and others to the life-changing power of improvisation.

BRENT: You know I believe that, no matter what our profession, we are all in the business of building relationships. That's why remembering names is important. Tell us how improv helps people strengthen relationships.

PATRICIA: Relationships are based on shared experiences. We make up stories, we enact dramas, we co-create. These brief, fictional activities make up a shared history. This history gives us a shared past. Improv teaches respect and listening. And improv teaches and models how to make mistakes, fail cheerfully, and develop tolerance for others' ways of working. All of this is foundational in healthy relationships.

BRENT: Beautiful insights. A former Stanford colleague of yours, the late Clifford Nass, maintained that the key elements of team building are "identification" and "interdependence." Sounds like that's what improv offers face to face.

PATRICIA: In this age of perpetual digital connection, there is an ongoing need for human connection. No matter how many likes we get on social media, nothing substitutes for being in the same room with a person and having a conversation or playing together.

BRENT: No question that technology offers a powerful supplement to our relationships, but it's not a replacement for it.

PATRICIA: I sense a deep longing for ways that we can be together without special equipment, training, or physical ability. Improv provides a safe crucible for being human.

BRENT: When I lead memory workshops, I bring in improv activities to get colleagues to interact more playfully.

PATRICIA: Successful teams know how to do more than work together. They are also good at play. Playing together flexes the muscles of cooperation and mutual respect. Teams come to "know each other" as players. In play, the rules of leading and following vary. Improv play teaches shared control, heightened listening, mutual respect, and the capacity to turn mistakes into winning moves.

BRENT: Setting each other up to succeed is an asset anywhere.

PATRICIA: There's a saying tossed around in improv to "make your partner look good." We don't do or say things that undermine or contradict others. We look for ways to support and encourage our partner and show them off in a good light. We accept offers and build upon them. We are choosing to cooperate rather than compete.

BRENT: The kind of mental agility that improv promotes is a health benefit. Now that humans are living longer, we need to stay healthier longer. Interestingly, improv activities can actually strengthen our relationships with Alzheimer's patients. Can you explain this?

PATRICIA: Yes, that's true. There's little to be gained from contradicting someone with Alzheimer's. Incorporating the behaviors we've been talking about can better the quality of the interactions, even with someone who is no longer the same.

BRENT: Thank you, Patricia. Improv does make the world a better place.

PATRICIA: Yes, and anyone can do it!

One of Patricia's favorite ice-breaker exercises is the Eye Contact Game, which she learned from fellow Stanford improviser Dan Klein. She explains it below.

Ask all players to stand in a circle. Take a moment for everyone to just look around and notice who is there. Then give this instruction:

Look around the circle and make eye contact with someone else. Once the two of you notice "we've made eye contact," then change places in the circle with that person. Once in your new position, look around to make eye contact with someone else. Change places in the circle. Keep on doing this until I say stop.

I do this for about 6-10 minutes, sometimes less. When we are back to the circle, I ask them to say something about that moment when they make eye contact and *know* they are now partnered. There is a small "aha" moment when we both acknowledge each other. I use this awareness to talk about the value of our taking the time to really *connect* with each other. Eye contact allows you and me to be on the same page momentarily. It's recognition.

You can use this game to discuss cultural differences. In Japan, for example, direct eye contact is considered a bit rude or aggressive. In Western culture, it is a high status move to hold eye contact.

It's useful to have players talk about their experience of this game. It's common to feel a little embarrassed when we make eye contact. It's personal and it's not uncommon to feel vulnerable when opening to someone, especially a stranger.

33.

CLOWNING AROUND—
SERIOUSLY!—
WITH AKRON WATSON

October 2017

Acharismatic Broadway actor explains how he gets his lines off the page and into his body.

You may recognize this leading man from the revival of *The Color Purple* on Broadway; regional theater productions of *Dream Girls, Smokey Joe's Café*, and *Bengal Tiger at the Baghdad Zoo*; or on television in season 6 of "American Idol" or "Friday Night Lights."

I was fortunate enough to meet Akron Watson after a performance of the hilarious farce *The Play That Goes Wrong*, in which he plays Trevor, the distracted sound and lighting operator mildly obsessed with Duran Duran. The guard at the stage door warned me that only a few of the actors would be coming out; most were either "getting food or physical therapy," much-needed recovery after a physically demanding show. Akron emerged buoyant and unscathed and was kind enough to answer my questions about memorization and character.

BRENT: Thanks for talking with me, Akron! What makes learning a role for *The Play That Goes Wrong* more challenging than for other shows you've been in?

AKRON: Nothing. It's still the same job. Knowing your lines, knowing your cues, and knowing what you want from the lines—the reasons and intention behind them.

BRENT: What specific training do you draw on for this play, in which professional actors are playing amateur actors playing stock characters?

AKRON: Clown. In rehearsals we were taught and trained about two types of clowns: Whiteface, the serious smart clown, and Auguste, the clumsy joking buffoon. All the characters in our show are different versions of these clowns. So, we improv-ed with that in mind.

BRENT: Knowing that helps me see the characters in a clearer way. What can you share about the dynamics of the ensemble?

AKRON: We play it seriously. We don't try to be funny or make fun of ourselves. The comedy comes from the pain and anguish we experience trying to get it right.

BRENT: Yes, it is one calamity after another. Actors convincingly blank on their lines, miss cues, get knocked out, or need to navigate around breaking props and collapsing sets.

AKRON: The goal is to get it right every night, which makes it funnier that it always goes wrong.

BRENT: I teach college communications courses and find that students are often resistant to memorization. What advice do you have for students who need to memorize a script or speech?

AKRON: Underline the verbs and make them sound different than all the other words. Speak the speech with the sound of the verbs heightened. Eventually that will create a rhythm that your brain will latch on to. It's also fun.

BRENT: Right, verbs are the action words and deserve heightened emphasis. In fact, the first speech I assign in class requires each student to identify three verbs that reflect his or her passion and develop them into a talk. What else do you recommend?

AKRON: Speak the speech in different environments: in an elevator, on the phone, at the grocery store, on the toilet, at the park. Also writing it down with your own handwriting helps.

BRENT: Absolutely. Physical reinforcement is the best.

AKRON: The point is, get them off the page and into your body.

BRENT: Wonderful advice! Thanks so much for your time, Akron. I really appreciate your sharing your knowledge. Keep breaking legs!

AKRON: Thanks for coming to the show!

34.
_____

CHRIS SAMS SINGS THE PRAISES OF HIS FAVORITE IMPROV GAME
May 2017

An experienced improvisation coach reveals how a simple game unifies a team in remarkable ways.

A proud member of San Francisco–based Bay Area TheatreSports (BATS) since 2005, Chris Sams is a highly skilled improvisational performer and training facilitator. Chris catalyzes teams to develop more innovative professionals and business leaders. He has led workshops focusing on a range of business skills, such as communication, adaptability, navigating change, creativity, leadership, presence, storytelling, collaboration, building trust, and enhancing team dynamics. Chris and I worked together for three years at BATS and had great fun playing word games and challenging each other's memories. Chris has a special fondness for a game called Ball, which he uses at the beginning of improv training. Read on to understand how this game generates trust, cooperation, and communication among the participants.

BRENT: Great to reconnect with you, Chris.

CHRIS: Thanks for thinking of me. I'm happy to talk with you about Ball.

BRENT: It is so basic and yet, as you have said, offers a surprising range of benefits.

CHRIS: True, few activities in the improviser's handbook model have as many parallels to the improvisational experience. The game gets its name from the soft squishy Koosh-like ball that the Bay Area improvisers bounce around in a volleyball circle, while together counting consecutively from one (one, two, three, etc.) each time any player makes contact with the ball.

BRENT: OK, so everyone is essentially playing a gentle game of volleyball by hitting this small beach ball to another person at random in the circle. There's no spiking or faking. The goal is to keep the ball in play as long as possible while everyone counts the number of hits together.

CHRIS: Correct. The process continues until the ball hits the stage floor or ground. Then the counting stops. Usually it's my practice to have the players cheer when that happens, as play resumes back at once.

BRENT: I remember this. The goal is to celebrate failure and move forward from it. It is only a dropped ball, after all. The person who fumbled can do an exaggerated "circus bow," like a clown, and shout, "Woo hoo! I failed!" Everyone cheers and moves on to the next round. There's nothing to be gained from cowering in shame, groaning, and bringing the mood of the room down.

CHRIS: Exactly. Ball offers up many benefits and life lessons. Embracing failure and letting go of mistakes is a big one. We don't blame ourselves or others if the ball falls. We instead look to the future of possibility. We take ourselves less seriously. We let go of blame.

BRENT: Beautifully stated. Let's go through some of the other benefits.

CHRIS: It's a strong physical warm-up for the improvisers. The players move around and get into their bodies. It's also a strong vocal warm-up and allows the players to work their vocal projection.

BRENT: Ball is deceptively simple. There really is a lot going on.

CHRIS: Ball promotes presence and awareness. Players must be totally in the moment, reacting and responding to their environment. There's also a strong sense of connection. Players notice each other, pass the ball to each other, notice who hasn't had the ball in a while, etc.

BRENT: Improv, like ballroom dancing, is one of the most holistic exercises one can do. It fosters physical exercise, mental agility, and social connectedness.

CHRIS: Yes, there is unity and ensemble. By counting in unison, players increase their connection and support a common goal. Even if they aren't making contact, they are part of the energy and contribution that propels the team forward.

BRENT: That's right, because everyone is participating by counting out loud, watching, listening, and anticipating. Ball is an excellent exercise to begin any workshop with. It gets people more in sync with each other. It makes them keener listeners and more likely to be supportive of others' ideas.

CHRIS: Ball is about teamwork and cooperation. There isn't a competitive spirit of us versus them; we are all a team and succeed as a team. If competitive, we are only competing with ourselves.

BRENT: These are the core tenets of improv: set each other up to succeed, make your partner look good, and fail good-naturedly.

CHRIS: Practice and ritual also come into play. If done consistently, we improve our craft, skills, and abilities, and have a common activity to build our troupe.

BRENT: Thank you so much for sharing your insights, Chris. I hope our interview gets Ball circulating more in the outside world. Improv really does make the world a better place.

CHRIS: I think so, too. It's been a pleasure.

FOREIGN AND TECHNICAL LANGUAGE

35.
*Joe Medeiros on Memorizing Foreign
Language Monologues*

36.
*Jenna Gavigan on Science and
Sexuality Off-Broadway*

35.

JOE MEDEIROS ON MEMORIZING FOREIGN LANGUAGE MONOLOGUES

December 2015

This resourceful artist shows us how to memorize in a language we don't know and how disruptions can actually be gifts.

Joseph Medeiros is an actor and poet in New York City. He is the founder of The Study, a space focused on process and inspiration. His goal is to make art a potent and important part of our life experience.

BRENT: What's the most demanding role you ever had to prepare for in terms of memorization?

JOE: One of the trickiest pieces of text I've had to memorize was a short monologue in Italian. I don't know Italian, so I looked it up and translated all the words and thought that would be enough. But as I was memorizing, I realized I was trying to do it more by rote, by the sounds of the words, rather than by meaning. I couldn't think in English and keep track of what was coming out of my mouth in Italian without a lot of pauses and thinking and literally translating.

BRENT: That sounds like a three-ring circus going on in your head. And you had to be in character, too.

JOE: Exactly. This wasn't even taking into account the fact that I had to *act* the words as well, and have a deep emotional and visceral connection to the words as they were coming out of my mouth. Also, while I was saying the words in Italian, other actors in the scene were translating into English, phrase by phrase, so I was constantly being hit with my native language, which only made my brain want to ditch the foreign Italian sounds and grab on to what was familiar and easier for it.

BRENT: So how did you make it work?

JOE: My delivery at this point was choppy and not terribly compelling. So, being a bit of an amateur philologist, my solution was to divorce the words from their English counterparts in my head by taking every word of the monologue and pulling it apart and discovering, or uncovering, its etymology, thus creating a personal connection and relationship with each word on its own terms. Almost like taking each one out for a coffee date, asking it where it's from, about its family, what it does for a living, and what its hopes and dreams are.

BRENT: As a linguist myself, this actually seems very appealing. Share an example of a word's back story.

JOE: One of the first pieces of the monologue had the phrase "La supplico," which has translations like "I beseech you" or "I beg you." Not helpful. But I took the word apart and found that it was made up of the Latin prefix *sub-*, which means "under, at the feet of, before." The second part of the word comes from the Latin verb *plicare*, meaning "fold, bend, or roll up." So the word "supplico," this *supplication*, becomes an act of folding oneself at another's feet, putting oneself below another, asking to be rolled into the actions of another while allowing them to be in the superior position. "I humble myself to you and ask you to take actions on my behalf, for our wills to be knit together, and I bow to you, acknowledge that I can't do this on my own, and ask this favor of you." Now that's a word that can be acted!

BRENT: What beautiful, vivid imagery you teased out of that one small word.

JOE: It also gave something for my body to do. When I said that word in the scene, I bowed my head ever so slightly, and had my hands a little in front of me with my palms facing out and up toward the person. This word became an indicator for an entire relationship as well as a physical movement, a dance step. And this created an immediate visceral and emotional arising in my body.

BRENT: So did you wind up doing this for every word in the monologue?

JOE: Yes, I did, for every single word and, in the end, created a complex dance of meaning and movement, sound, sense, and action. So many words are rooted in very real, physical verbs, and the weaving together of the text in this way makes memorization almost a non-issue, nearly a byproduct of the process.

BRENT: Ralph Waldo Emerson said that every word is a frozen metaphor. For example, the English word "pearl" comes from the Latin "perula," which means "little pear." You found and distilled the poetry inside each word, and leveraged it for your interpretation. Bravo!

JOE: In performance my body danced a series of sounds, which happened to be Italian. And then the sounds themselves became a dance with my voice, literally with the muscles that move the breath and the vocal articulators, a song as a dance. There was no chance that I was going to forget those words.

BRENT: I suppose you could do this for Shakespeare, Beckett, and any other work with challenging language.

JOE: Yes, I've done this for text in English, too, and it works just as well.

BRENT: What tricks do you have to stay focused on stage? How do you tune out audience chatter and ringing cell phones, or even backstage distractions?

JOE: That is such a great question! You know, I don't think it's necessary to tune anything out. I think the best way to deal with "unhelpful" distractions is to let them in, acknowledge them, and even let them affect what you're doing if, in the moment, it feeds the moment.

BRENT: Really!? Help me understand how you do that.

JOE: Now, I don't mean completely break the performance, but there is a way to split your focus for a moment and become an *observer* while you are doing. I first became aware of this as a dancer. Ideally, when I'm dancing, I like to rehearse until the movements feel obvious and there's no need to think about what comes next, or any sort of logistical things. That way, when I perform, I can put all my focus on *dancing*, on being expressive through movement.

BRENT: I love how free and liberating this sounds. Still, what about focus and concentration?

JOE: This is the ideal, but there are always moments when the more analytical side has to come in; maybe I wasn't quite on balance for that turn, or I came down from that jump in a strange way and need to adjust, or another dancer is not quite on their mark, and if I don't adjust, one of us is going to get kicked. All of those things are a matter of safety and it behooves the dancer to be able to deal with these events, possibly make physical adjustments, but maintain the expressive continuity and integrity of the performance.

BRENT: So, distraction can keep you on your toes, so to speak.

JOE: A distraction or something unexpected puts us into a heightened state where emotions and pure impulse are given more space. Why try to ignore this kind of gift if it can be of service to you as an actor?

BRENT: You do make it sound like a gift. What about the irritation of the ringing cell phone coming from the audience?

JOE: Now, I wasn't there for this, but it's one of my favorite stories: an actress, whose name I can't remember, was playing Medea, and during one of her big arguments with Jason, a cell phone went off in the audience. Bad timing, right? So she paused for just a moment, then turned slowly, and continued her vituperation to Jason while looking at the audience member whose phone had gone off! So the play continued, but the obvious intrusion wasn't ignored.

BRENT: What brilliant thinking on the spot!

JOE: Like you, I hate that moment as an audience member when a cell phone goes off and you get pulled away from the play, even though it's still going on and the actors are obviously aware of the ringing, but they're just continuing. Then the cell phone finally stops, and we're all a little annoyed, and we have to make an adjustment to re-engage and return to the play, and you swear you can almost see the actors breathe a sigh of relief.

BRENT: And the audience breathes a sigh of relief along with the actors.

JOE: But this actress playing Medea pulled the fictive circumstances together with the realities of the moment and created a beautiful, seamless theatrical moment that could have been missed if she'd chosen to ignore it. And anger is an obvious emotion that would come up in that situation. There are a lot of different things it could bring up in the actor: a sense of sadness at the interruption, a joyful sense of the absurdness of being onstage in the first place with a large group of people watching you, or something else entirely.

BRENT: When you put it that way, the intrusion almost becomes a welcome opportunity to create something new.

JOE: That's a good point. In theater there's this great tension, on the one hand, between the conservative values of repeatability, stability, and predictability that are embodied in set lines, choreography, blocking, lighting cues, and everything that makes the structure; and on the other hand, the opportunity to embrace the reality of the unpredictable, the ever-changing, the fact that the performance you are doing will never happen again, the audience will never be the same, and you'll never be the same because you aren't the same from one day to the next or even from one moment to the next.

BRENT: That's quite a paradox. It's amazing that the show goes on at all. What do you think makes it all come together?

JOE: The tension gets resolved by using the set elements of the structure. They oppose each other, but they need each other so that the piece can be seen and experienced and enjoyed.

BRENT: Beautifully put, Joe. Thank you for opening up your heart and mind and sharing your perspective. Your creative process has changed the way I'll look at acting.

JOE: It's been my pleasure.

36.

JENNA GAVIGAN ON SCIENCE AND SEXUALITY OFF-BROADWAY

May 2016

The stage and screen actress explains her preparation for a role in a provocative new play about sexual identity.

Jenna Gavigan has appeared in a Broadway revival of *Gypsy* alongside Bernadette Peters and in popular television series, such as "The Good Wife," "Boardwalk Empire," and "House of Cards." Jenna just wrapped up an off-Broadway run of the play *Straight*, about a bisexual love triangle that challenges assumptions about stereotypes and sexual autonomy. She plays the conflicted protagonist's female love interest, Emily, a Ph.D. candidate in genetics and bioinformatics. We spoke after a performance.

BRENT: What is the most challenging role you've ever had to prepare for in terms of memorization?

JENNA: Oh, my. Well, when I first got the script for *Straight*, I'll admit I was a bit overwhelmed. I think it's the most words I've ever had to memorize for a job. I was especially concerned with Emily's scientific jargon because I knew I had to not only memorize it, but seem like I knew what I was talking about.

BRENT: It would be a lot to expect an actor to have expertise in this field. How did you approach this?

JENNA: So for that, I spoke with our writers, and they explained to me what Emily actually does in terms of working towards her Ph.D.—and curing cancer! Once I understood her (very intense) work, I had an easier time memorizing. And because it was just the three of us [Tom Sullivan, Jake Epstein, and myself] in the play, rehearsal from 10 to 6 every day was more than enough time to memorize the play as a whole.

BRENT: Sounds like duration and repetition were your best friends. What about memorizing for television?

JENNA: I had to memorize a poem by Dante Gabriel Rossetti for "Boardwalk Empire." Because there's no time for rehearsal for most television, I just kept going over and over it. (Luckily, I had a little time with it. Thanks, "Boardwalk" writers!) I think it's now in my mind forever. There's nothing like knowing a whole crew will be staring at you to motivate memorization!

BRENT: Right, so let's add urgency to that list! What sticks with you from your school days?

JENNA: I'll say that while I don't remember all of what I studied in school, I remember a lot of blocking lines from past shows. *The Moo Cow* and *Broadway, Broadway* choreography is permanently planted in my brain. I suspect Emily's lines will be as well. I think the difference is that I wasn't always in love with what I was memorizing in school, but I'm ever in love with my job.

BRENT: A lot of actors I talk with mention muscle memory—they repeat lines out loud and even record them and play them back incessantly. Do you do that?

JENNA: For auditions, I find that running lines out loud with a partner helps a lot. If I can't do that, I will record myself reading all of the lines and then listen to them while I do something mindless like folding laundry.

BRENT: Let's go back to your role as Emily in *Straight*. Tell me more about your interaction with the writers to understand the complex fields of genetics and bioinformatics. You certainly delivered the scientific processes and jargon with convincing expertise.

JENNA: Thank you for saying I spoke with conviction. That was my goal! Emily is nothing if not educated and passionate about her work, so I needed to respect that. I owe that to researching every scientific term Emily spoke, as well as discussing it with one of our writers, Scott Elmegreen. He was a good teacher. I guess a rule of thumb is: don't try to memorize something without actually understanding it at a basic level.

BRENT: Makes sense. The audience would definitely pick up on that. OK, last question: do you have a favorite story about forgetting a line and having to get back on track?

JENNA: Well, during our first preview, I called an offstage character (Ben's friend, Tim), CHRIS. And then I recovered with, "No. You're Chris. I meant Tim. You know, crazy Tim." Improvisation and listening will always help get back on track, as do helpful costars. No show is ever going to be "perfect" and certainly no audition will be "perfect," so just staying in the story and knowing the wants and needs of the characters will always keep things grounded.

BRENT: Nice recovery, without drawing undue attention to the line. Thanks so much for sharing your stories.

JENNA: Thank you!

DOUBLING UP

37.

KENDAL HARTSE ON LEARNING MULTIPLE ROLES FOR A SINGLE SHOW

September 2016

A Broadway actor talks about preparation for dual roles and the rewards of collaborative improvisation.

Kendal Hartse and I met a decade ago at Boston Conservatory, where she was a stand-out in the musical theater department, and I headed up marketing and communications. It's no surprise that Kendal went on to settle in New York City and appear on Broadway in shows like *Rodgers and Hammerstein's Cinderella* and *On A Clear Day You Can See Forever.* Equally at home acting, singing, or dancing, Kendal has also performed on tour and in regional theater in the roles of Sally Bowles in *Cabaret,* Yitzhak in *Hedwig and the Angry Inch,* Nellie in *Floyd Collins,* and Baptista/Lucentio in *Taming of the Shrew.* It was a delight to catch up with her by email for this interview.

BRENT: Wonderful to reconnect with you, Kendal! Tell me, what was the most challenging role you ever had to prepare for in terms of memorization?

KENDAL: I think the most challenging role I had to prepare for in terms of memorization was probably when I played both Lucentio *and* Baptista in *Taming of the Shrew* at the Virginia Stage Company. It always seems harder for me to memorize when I'm working on multiple characters. If I have one character to worry about, I have an easier time committing the text to memory since it follows more logically.

BRENT: Yeah, two very different characters in the same show definitely counts as a challenge!

KENDAL: When you jump back and forth between two characters—who sometimes have polar opposite goals and wants—it can be tricky to keep the sequencing in your head and follow the line of the story. This production had the added challenge of learning music both vocally and instrumentally (violin and electric guitar). Add all of this to only a two-and-a-half-week rehearsal period, and you've got a challenge!

BRENT: So, how did you approach what amounts to a four-part role?

KENDAL: I came at it by working on each character individually. I memorized all of Lucentio before I started memorizing for Baptista. When I'm faced with learning multiple tracks in a show—like this case, or as an offstage cover, or an onstage understudy—I like to take them one at a time. I think it's easier that way and also less confusing.

BRENT: Tackling them separately makes sense. What about your method of both speaking and listening your lines?

KENDAL: For this show, as in most shows, I made a recording of the text that I would listen to when I was walking around town or riding the train. When I was at home, I'd speak the text with the recording while looking at the physical page, and then without the page, and then without the recording. This helped me come into rehearsals virtually off book (something I like to do), and the rest of the memorization fell into place easily once there was blocking.

BRENT: A number of actors have told me that commitment to character facilitates memorization. How has this helped you master your lines?

KENDAL: Commitment to character is hugely helpful in mastering lines. I think that if you are in character and thinking within the world of the play, the text usually makes sense. Knowing how the character thinks, speaks, and moves makes saying her text logical. When I played Sally

Bowles in *Cabaret,* I found this commitment incredibly helpful, especially since I had to use an accent.

BRENT: Interesting. Most people might think that an accent is an extra burden, not an aid to memorization.

KENDAL: Just as I find it easier to learn words in songs—the melody makes the words so much simpler to memorize—an accent is a great help in memorization. It gives the text a cadence and a rhythm. In the case of Sally, how she spoke was *so* specific that the memorization came easily.

BRENT: Have you ever gone up on your lines during a performance?

KENDAL: I have absolutely gone up on my lines in a show. I've heard people refer to it as "going into the white room," which is exactly what it feels like. You're going along, talking, saying your lines, when suddenly—POOF!—everything disappears. The text is gone, the stage is gone, your scene partner is gone. You are just in that white room with no idea how you got there or how to get out.

BRENT: Yikes, how do you get back on track?

KENDAL: I'd say nine times out of ten, I snap back pretty quickly. If you just breathe, just take a deep breath, the text is usually right where you left it. Your brain and body know it; you just have to trust yourself. It feels like you were gone forever, but it's almost always just a few seconds. I've rarely, if ever, been so stranded and for so long that another actor had to jump in, but if your scene partner is really present with you, sometimes just looking at them and being present with them is enough to get you back on track.

BRENT: Sounds like you've had to do this for others.

KENDAL: I've occasionally had to help other actors in this situation. I memorize aurally, so I often know my scene partner's lines before I know my own. This helps me be able to repeat, ask questions, or maneuver around any dead air if someone seriously goes up.

BRENT: I've heard actors tend to know each other's lines almost through osmosis. Being present and attuned to the flow of a well-written show facilitates that.

KENDAL: To go back to commitment to character being helpful, I once had a situation where an actor I was performing with missed a big entrance, but my fellow actors and I were able to improvise an entire scene in her absence thanks to being in character and knowing all of the text really well. We just made something up!

BRENT: That is phenomenal! OK, final question. Any final advice for anyone needing to learn a script or speech?

KENDAL: If it's helpful, my technique for memorization is to do a combination of listening and repetition. For longer scenes, I like to listen to recordings, and for long monologues, I like to go line by line and sometimes word by word, stacking the monologue up in my brain. For example, "Oh for a muse of fire that would ascend the brightest heaven of invention" becomes: Oh. Oh for. Oh for a. Oh for a muse. Oh for a muse of fire, etc.

BRENT: We started with Shakespeare, so let's end with him. Kendal, I greatly appreciate your time. Thanks for sharing your process with my readers.

KENDAL: Thank you so much for asking me to do an interview.

38.

KELLEY CURRAN ON PREPARING FOR THE ROLE OF ANNA KARENINA IN FOUR DAYS

November 2016

A Broadway actress masters a new character during the day in record time—while performing the lead in a Shakespeare play at night.

Fresh off her run as the levelheaded sister Elinor in a wildly engaging production of *Sense & Sensibility*, Kelley Curran exudes a warm, grounded air, much like her character. Regularly performing on main stages here in New York and at such distinguished regional theaters as Shakespeare & Company, Shakespeare Theatre of DC, and the Guthrie in Minneapolis, Kelley has received the Joe Callaway Award for Best Performance by an Actress in a Classic Play in NYC and earned nominations from the Drama League and Princess Grace Awards. We spoke after one of the final performances of the Jane Austen–based play.

BRENT: Kelley, thank you so much for talking with me.

KELLEY: I'm so happy you were able to make the show, and even more thrilled you enjoyed it as much as you did. Indeed, it has been a whirlwind nearing the end of the run of *Sense & Sensibility*.

BRENT: Oh, yes! Speaking of whirlwind, with all the constant character, costume, and set changes that the actors were taxed with in this production, I would have thought this would have been one of the most challenging roles you ever had to prepare for. But apparently that distinction goes to your portrayal of Anna Karenina out in Oregon.

KELLEY: Preparing to play the title role in an adaptation of *Anna Karenina* in four days time, while I was performing the lead role of a Shakespeare play in the evenings, was without a doubt the most challenging task I've ever faced in terms of memorization, and perhaps in terms of my entire career as an actress.

BRENT: How did this come about?

KELLEY: I was working at Portland Center Stage playing the role of Imogen in Shakespeare's *Cymbeline*. The run of *Cymbeline* was winding down (we had just seven performances left) when the artistic director of the same theater asked me on a Tuesday if I would step in and take over the role of Anna Karenina in a world premiere stage adaptation that was being performed in the larger of the two performance spaces at the theater.

BRENT: Right, a world premiere that was set to open that very weekend. Flattering, but daunting!

KELLEY: The great challenge being that I would have to learn the text and all the blocking for *Anna Karenina* in four and a half days, and be ready to perform it that Sunday night, after a closing matinee of *Cymbeline* that afternoon.

BRENT: For some people, there's no better motivation than being pressed for time. How did you tackle the script?

KELLEY: Learning the text of Anna K. essentially just became the task of all my waking hours when I was outside of actual rehearsal for the play and my nightly performances of *Cymbeline*. I just put myself on an extremely regimented schedule, such that I woke five hours before rehearsal, memorized from the start of the play onward, rehearsed during the day, took an hour dinner break, memorized over dinner, performed the other play at night, came home, and continued the memorization process for two more hours before sleeping.

BRENT: That sounds intense, but necessary, given the compressed time frame.

KELLEY: My process for memorizing this particular time around (when I knew that I was so very limited) was very much by rote. I would learn one line, move on to the next, learn the next line, then go back, say the first and second lines out loud, then learn the third line, go back and say all three lines out loud, then learn the fourth line...and onward and onward. It was tedious and by rote, but I would learn each scene like this.

BRENT: What about working with other actors to cement your lines?

KELLEY: Once I'd learned my lines from each scene, I then had a volunteer from the theater available to me to speak the whole scene out loud over and over. Then I would move on to the next scene, and learn that in the same way.

BRENT: Both speaking and hearing the lines are excellent forms of reinforcement. Another is writing the lines by hand out for added visuals and muscle memory. You must have done that, too.

KELLEY: When my voice would get too tired to continue, or if I knew I needed to rest it, I would write the lines down with pen and paper, instead of speaking them. This way I was still forced to go word by word, thought by thought—and I could do it silently. This is a memorization technique I often use when I'm commuting on the train, or anywhere in public and I need to be learning lines. Rather than speaking them out loud and risking unnerving all the people around you, I'll write lines down to memorize them.

BRENT: I wish more train commuters were as considerate as you! Do you ever use any visualization and association techniques to master your lines, or is memorization for you largely character-driven?

KELLEY: Visualization as a tool for memorization sometimes does come into play as an actor, particularly if the text is on the poetic side, or filled with imagery. Personally, for me, memorization becomes deeply linked with the action of the play, and the action of the argument your character is making.

BRENT: Making compelling arguments is a hallmark of Jane Austen's strong, rational leading characters, of which Elinor is certainly one.

KELLEY: All communication is an effort to understand and be understood, so if I, as an actor, have a firm grasp of the argument my character is making, or what they need to express in any given moment, it becomes easier for me to remember what the words are that articulate that need.

BRENT: Absolutely. And when you fully embody your character, and the text is expertly written, the things your character can say and do follow a very logical thread.

KELLEY: I imagine the same is true for most public speaking—if you know the point you're trying to make and believe deeply in what you are saying, the words will be easier to remember because they will be the logical and inevitable conclusion of your thoughts and feelings on a subject. On stage, the words of the play (most of the time) are the articulation of the character's objective, whether opaque or transparent.

BRENT: That's very true for linear, sequential ideas in speeches as well as scripts. When a presenter like a politician or business leader has to tick off, say, ten disjointed concepts and provide additional facts, figures, and color, that's where some other creative memory techniques can come in handy.

KELLEY: That's really interesting! Well, thank you again for coming to see the play, and for telling me about your business. I hope this has been at all helpful or useful to you, Brent!

STAGE VS. TELEVISION

39.

JEREMY DAVIDSON ON EMOTIONAL HONESTY
April 2017

The stage and screen actor talks about his passion for performing in new plays—and much more.

Any serious viewer of television dramas such as "Law & Order," "Army Wives," "The Kill Point," "Brothers & Sisters," "NYPD Blue," and "Pan Am" will recognize this handsome actor. Jeremy Davidson is also known for his stage and film work, often with an emphasis on political history and social conscience. He and his wife, fellow actor Mary Stuart Masterson, founded the Storyhorse Documentary Theater, whose works explore and bring to vivid life the history of New York's Hudson Valley. Read on to learn about their fascinating mission, as well as Jeremy's approach to the differences between mastering roles for the stage and television.

BRENT: What would you say was the most demanding role you ever had to prepare for in terms of memorization?

JEREMY: I'd say the most challenging role (memorization-wise) that I've worked on was a one-man play called *Nijinsky's Last Dance*. It was written by Norman Allen and is based on the life and institutionalization of the Russian ballet dancer Vaslav Nijinsky. I played the role three times—initially at the Signature Theater in Washington, DC, and then again four years later at the Kennedy Center and Berkshire Theater Festival. The play—if my memory still serves me!—ran about 1 hour and 20 minutes without an intermission.

Brent: That's a long stretch! Do you have a general approach for learning a role?

JEREMY: For me, each role seems to have its own unique process; I don't always find it useful to commit my lines to memory in advance of rehearsals beginning, as I tend to feel more expansive creatively and more open to discovery if I first explore the world of a play through research and conversations with the other actors and director.

BRENT: So, get to know your character and his environment before digging into the specific lines.

JEREMY: Exactly. The more elusive thing to discover is how a character thinks, his motivations, physical rhythms, and where the need to say the words I have to say comes from. Ultimately, if I can find those things and somehow root them in my subconscious mind, it gives me a better chance at creating truthful behavior underneath the words.

BRENT: So how does all this relate to your mastering of the Nijinsky role?

JEREMY: For the Nijinsky play, I knew I would need to be physically free of the script in advance of rehearsal. I'm not a dancer, so my body also needed to try to learn the language of ballet as well. I was cast about a month before rehearsals started, so I tried to lock myself in a room and memorize five pages a day by rote—without any emotional choices to the words or lines or sections.

BRENT: Sounds practical but at odds with the deeper connections you prefer to explore.

JEREMY: Ultimately, I found it lonely working this way. I much prefer being able to work off other actors and having discoveries and impulses triggered by their choices in a scene. But then again, the isolation Nijinsky had to face was far more terrifying than what I had to deal with.

BRENT: Right, Nijinsky's final years were very sad, spent largely in the confinement of psychiatric hospitals.

JEREMY: Far more terrifying.

BRENT: Have you ever worked on a show with frequent rewrites, new material, and rearranged sequences? How do you keep the most recent version in your head and scrub the old one?

JEREMY: In the theater, I actually prefer working on new plays, which usually means you will get rewrites throughout rehearsals, previews, and up to opening night. And over the past ten years, I've really only worked on new plays. I love having access to the playwright in rehearsal. It's a luxury you don't get working on Tennessee Williams or Eugene O'Neill. Of course, if a scene isn't working, it can be a difficult conversation as to why—is it the writing that needs to change or is it the actors or is it a bit of both?

BRENT: It's a privilege to get to ask those questions directly.

JEREMY: So, when rewrites and cuts to the narrative come in, you can feel if there are suddenly jumps to the emotional logic you've built into a scene. And sometimes you do slip back into old drafts, but that's just the nature of theater.

BRENT: And where some of your most creative acting skills come into play to get the scene back on track.

JEREMY: One of the more interesting things a director once told me was how much better my performance was one night when the other actor forgot their lines. The director said I seemed to be "more present" when it happened. As difficult as that "compliment" was to take—I wanted to believe I was good every night in the role—it also made sense to me. I was forced to really listen to what was being said by the other actor, instead of taking for granted we were going to be on the same path the script and memory had laid out for us.

BRENT: The saying goes that mistakes are gifts. So yours was the chance to be more natural, if not vulnerable.

JEREMY: Relying on memory too much can lock us down into repeated behavior that isn't always free and spontaneous. And I guess losing track of that roadmap forced me to search for the words in a fresh way.

BRENT: How is working in television different?

JEREMY: In television, rewrites come every day. Some of the best writers and directors throw new lines at you, take to take. So you have to stay open to it and trust you understand the circumstance of the scene.

BRENT: Do you have a favorite example?

JEREMY: When I worked on "NYPD Blue" years ago, David Milch came in with a completely rewritten scene just minutes before we were going to shoot. But he's a terrific writer and his words are easy to memorize quickly. That's not to say you don't stress it in the moment; it's just that emotionally true writing is easy to memorize quickly for some reason.

BRENT: That makes perfect sense. The lines are easier to memorize the more they align with the character's personality or motivation. What are the main differences between television and the stage?

JEREMY: The most difficult dialogue to memorize (for me) is when a showrunner (or the network executives whispering over their shoulders) feel a need to remind the audience of events that happened in previous episodes and fill your dialogue with a lot of exposition. As an actor, it feels "heady," as if the lines are more motivated to the writer's need to explain plot or history to an audience than the character's need to share information with another character. The latter is a lot easier to commit to memory. But television and film really aren't actors' mediums; stories and performances are shaped and manipulated so much in the editing room. So, when you screw up a line on set—as frustrating as it is for everyone there—you can simply do another take. And if you never get it right, they'll either cut it out or have you come in and record the line in post-production. So, though the audience hears you say the line, the editor stays on the other actor while you say it—and nobody has to see your struggle.

BRENT: What other anecdotes would you like to share about getting into character and memorizing material?

JEREMY: Well, I hesitate to share this, as I don't want to sound overly precious about being an actor. Though I feel real lucky to make a living doing this, I don't always find it to be the most useful way to engage in the world. But I've come to believe that there is a stage in the creative process that is a conversation with our subconscious, or spirit, or some higher part of ourselves. And physical repetition can unlock the door to that place. There was a scene in a play I did where I had to lift another actor up against the wall, pull back my fist, and punch him in the face. When we moved into tech rehearsal, I had to repeat that gesture about 50 times, making sure the movements were specific and had the appearance of real violence without endangering the other actor.

BRENT: That sounds intense!

JEREMY: Anyway, that night, I had a dream I was being attacked. And the person in my dream was grabbing my leg. As I did in the play, I jumped up, pulled back my fist and prepared to punch the person. But all of a sudden, my wife's voice broke into my dream, saying, "Whoa, whoa, whoa!" When I opened my eyes to reality, I realized she had been shaking my leg to wake me up, and in response, I had jumped up in bed and pulled back my fist, preparing to punch her.

BRENT: Yikes! Scary, and yet a testament to how deeply an actor embodies his character, physically and emotionally.

JEREMY: Yeah, it wouldn't have been a great moment for our marriage.

BRENT: You and I run into each other at storytelling events in the Hudson Valley. One of the things you do with your acting is bring history to life with your own theater company, the Storyhorse Documentary Theater.

JEREMY: Storyhorse Documentary Theater is a project my wife Mary Stuart Masterson and I started here in the Hudson Valley. We record people's stories, transcribe them, and then, using historical documents and other primary sources, shape them into live multimedia theater pieces where actors read the stories surrounded by a projection and sound design. We've produced three pieces so far: *The Little Things* is about a family in Poughkeepsie who lost their 17-year-old son to Lyme Disease; *Good Dirt,* a collection of Hudson Valley farm families; and *The Kept Private,* a narrative about slavery and race in our town through the Revolutionary War pension application of a black farmer in the town of Milan.

BRENT: I saw *The Kept Private,* and it chilled me to the core—in a good way! It made me think of a play I saw a decade ago, *The Exonerated,* about death row inmates wrongfully convicted and whose sentences were eventually overturned. *The Kept Private* reminds us of social injustices that took a long time to make right. And you cast a diverse line-up of first-rate actors who bring their characters very much to life. What's coming up next?

JEREMY: Our next piece focuses on a remarkable cold case in Rhinebeck from 1949. These local stories have given us a chance to bring our own work to the place where we're raising our kids. And a useful way for us to be a part of the collective spirit and history of the Hudson Valley.

BRENT: Thanks, Jeremy. I look forward to seeing it. Thank you for being so generous with your time, words, and experiences.

JEREMY: My pleasure. I hope you found this useful.

40.

AUDREY RAPOPORT ON BETTER LIVING THOUGH IMPROV

May 2017

Script or no script, this comedic actor is at the top of her game.

Audrey Rapoport—actor, improviser, writer, and teacher—has been called "one of those great, great character actresses" and "uproariously funny." Audrey is a master of comedic physicality. Whether stealing a scene in a play or bringing quirky characters to life at a story slam, her facial contortions, body language from nuanced to outrageous, and deft vocal modulations drive the public wild. Audrey and I met in the Hudson Valley at a staged reading of Yasmina Reza's adults-behaving-badly comedy *God of Carnage*. Audrey cut her acting chops with the Los Angeles–based improv troupe The Groundlings and reveals how that experience shaped her life.

BRENT: How has improvisational theater training made you more aware of your surroundings?

AUDREY: I went to film school, so my "formal" acting training began at The Groundlings, the world-famous improvisation school in LA. It turned out to be an absolutely fantastic foundation. Every actor, indeed every person alive, should take an improv class. I took many. I performed as a member of The Groundlings for many years, and today I teach comedy improv at School of Visual Arts and Marymount Manhattan College in NYC.

BRENT: You don't have to sell me on the benefits of improv! It's boosted my ability to think more creatively and faster on my feet. But you're the pro. Tell me what it does for you.

AUDREY: Improv forces you to be in the moment and to react immediately to what you're given. You also learn to utilize the eyes in the back of your head, to be aware of everything that everyone is doing, including the audience.

BRENT: What about when you're working with a script?

AUDREY: When working with scripted material, whether it be a sketch or a more complex piece, I am a stickler for maintaining the integrity of the words on the page, but life isn't perfect and shit goes down.

BRENT: So true! How do you get back on track if your mind goes blank on a line?

AUDREY: At that point, it becomes all about eye contact and breathing. Someone on stage is bound to find the way back in, and then everyone else can follow along.

BRENT: Where does memorization fall in your process of learning a character?

AUDREY: I prefer to memorize lines later in the game, after a healthy amount of rehearsing. It helps me to first understand the logic of the scene, and then start working on the blocking. Your head's attached to your body, and your body's attached to your head, so where one goes, the other follows. I don't always have that luxury, and in some cases, a director will ask that actors be off book very early in the process.

BRENT: Then what? How do you go about learning the material?

AUDREY: In those cases, I just sit down with the script and memorize it a chunk at a time. Then back to the beginning, always adding a bit more. Every time I screw up, I start from the beginning. Sometimes there's a difficult section, or a series of words that are challenging. I usually use a mnemonic device of the first letter of the words to remember that it's alphabetical.... Or keep a phrase in the back of my mind.

BRENT: For example?

AUDREY: Like if I need to remember the line "harried and dramatic," I will think "Harley Davidson."

BRENT: Great visual!

AUDREY: I fear it's only a matter of time before I blurt out my mnemonic phrase instead of the actual line. But as I said, I like to stick to the script word for word. I despise paraphrasing and working with actors who do that can be very—how can I put this diplomatically....tricky. Let's go with tricky.

BRENT: Ha! You've also had parts in soap operas, a very specific genre. That's something I talked with Jeremy Davidson about. What's that like for you?

AUDREY: Soap operas pose particular challenges because the dialogue is very repetitive. Each episode is made up of several scenes that are basically the same, but the words change slightly. The blocking has nothing to do with character motivation and everything to do with camera angles.

BRENT: That's certainly a departure from the way things work on stage. So I'm guessing that you stick to exactly what's in the script.

AUDREY: I never feel comfortable paraphrasing when I'm just guesting on a show. I leave that for the regulars. I don't get mad at *them*. I get envious, but not mad. I'm not a monster.

BRENT: What was one of your favorite roles in a soap opera?

AUDREY: One time I played an oncologist, and I had tons of medical jargon to memorize. Every one of my scenes ended with me saying, "We'll know more after the surgery."

BRENT: Even with that line, you still had to understand the dialogue in order to deliver it with conviction. The stage actress Jenna Gavigan told me that she spent time with the writers to fully understand her lines when she played a geneticist. You may have done something similar.

AUDREY: I managed to not butcher the dialogue, but I may have killed the patient. I'm not telling!

BRENT: Good thing it's all just make-believe. No real jury would convict you! Thanks so much for your insights and good humor, Audrey. You are a delight to talk with.

AUDREY: Glad I could give you answers that are coherent. Thank you!

41.

JOHN BENJAMIN HICKEY ON THE SCIENCE AND CHEMISTRY OF CHARACTER

June 2017

A Tony Award–winning actor upends the conventional wisdom of learning and understanding.

John Benjamin Hickey just wrapped up the Broadway revival of *Six Degrees of Separation*, in which he starred alongside Allison Janney. In addition to winning a Tony for his 2011 performance in *The Normal Heart*, Hickey has a long career in stage, film, and television work. You may have seen him on Broadway in *Love! Valour! Compassion!*, *Cabaret*, or *The Crucible*; or on TV in "Alias," "Law & Order," "Brothers & Sisters," "Heartland," "Law & Order: Los Angeles," and "Modern Family."

John signed my playbill at the stage door of *Six Degrees* and asked why I had a reporter's notebook flipped open. Replying to my question about how he memorizes dialogue, he exceeded my expectations. Here are the fruits of our exchange.

BRENT: What is the most challenging role you've ever tackled in terms of memorization?

JOHN: In all honesty, it's whatever I am working on at the time. And the older you get, the truer that becomes. But it also depends on the part.

BRENT: What part are you thinking of?

JOHN: A couple of years ago, I played a theoretical nuclear physicist on a wonderful TV show called "Manhattan." It was about the people who built the first atom bomb, and the stuff I had to learn was very...scientific.

And believe me, I did not become an actor because I was a science whiz. That was very difficult material to learn, and I swear sometimes it felt like I was learning it phonetically. Not really, but it is a fact that in some cases if you just learn it, you also begin to learn what it means.

BRENT: Don't sweat it. Rocket science does not come easily to most people!

JOHN: I know they always say you have to understand what you're saying before you actually learn it, but that's not always the case.

BRENT: It makes sense that the more effort you put into learning the material, the better you come to understand its internal logic.

JOHN: It's interesting, this has me thinking about the difference between film and theatre.

BRENT: Which is...?

JOHN: Memorization is so different in television than it is in the theater. In television, you often times get the script pages the day *before* you film it, and then, of course, you shoot it, go home, and at the end of the day, the whole thing starts over again, with brand new pages. So there is a lot of cramming involved.

BRENT: And in the theater...?

JOHN: In the theater, you have....time. You have rehearsal, you have repetition. Allison Janney—with whom I co-starred in the recent Broadway revival of *Six Degrees of Separation*—and I had the luxury of being old friends and very comfortable with each other, so when we discovered we would be in the same town some months before rehearsal began, I would go over to her house every weekend, and we would make screwdrivers and work on our lines. I don't know if the vodka helped, but the working together to learn John Guare's amazingly dense and dexterous dialogue sure did. And all we would do is just read it to each other, again and again and again.

BRENT: Having seen you both in the show, I can attest to your chemistry. You were certainly believable as a longtime married couple.

JOHN: Lucky for us it's such a great play, so we never got tired of it.

BRENT: In my interview with Kate Wetherhead and Greg Mullavey, they concurred that good, strong writing makes a play easier to memorize. As does sheer repetition.

JOHN: It's all about repetition. And rehearsal is, of course, everything. Figuring out *why* you're saying what you're saying, and how that is manifested physically in the blocking, those are all keys to remembering. Hamlet said it best: "Suit the word to the action, the action to the word."

BRENT: It's hard to argue with Shakespeare. I always like to ask actors if they have a favorite story about getting back on track after a forgotten line or unexpected occurrence. What is yours?

JOHN: In our very first preview of *Six Degrees of Separation,* we were all so nervous. Allison's character has a big plate of pasta on stage, and one of the penne noodles fell off the plate and onto the floor. The entire audience saw it fall, and without missing a beat, she reached down, picked it up, said, "Three second rule!!" and promptly ate it. It was a line worthy of John Guare, which is saying a lot. It's as good an example as any I can think of as to why she is my hero.

BRENT: What a sweet story, and a testament to her ability to stay in character. Thank you so much for talking with me. I look forward to seeing you again, on stage or anywhere.

JOHN: Thank you for coming to the show!

BIBLIOGRAPHY

Barton, Robert and Dal Vera, Rocco. *Voice: Onstage and Off* (Second Edition). London: Routledge (2011).

Black, David. *The Magic of the Theater: Behind the Scenes with Today's Leading Actors*. New York: Macmillan Publishing Company (1993).

Gabler, Neal. *Life the Movie: How Entertainment Conquered Reality*. New York: Alfred A. Knopf (1998).

Guskin, Harold. *How to Stop Acting*. New York: Farrar, Straus and Giroux (2003).

Lowe, Rob. *Love Life*. New York: Simon & Schuster (2014).

Moore, Sonia. *The Stanislavski Method: The Professional Training of an Actor*. New York: The Viking Press (1960).

Morris, Eric and Hotchkis, Joan. *No Acting Please*. Ermor Enterprises (1995).

Reeves, Byron and Nass, Clifford. *The Media Equation: How People Treat Computers, Television, and New Media Like Real People and Places*. Stanford: Center for the Study of Language and Information (1996).

Sondheim, Stephen. Lyrics from "Being Alive" from *Company*. New York: Columbia 30th Street Studios (1970).

The Low Anthem. Lyrics from "Charlie Darwin." Bella Union / Nonesuch (2008).

Yates, Frances A. *The Art of Memory*. The University of Chicago Press (1966).

ACKNOWLEDGMENTS

Very special thanks to all the creative geniuses interviewed here who were so generous with their time and wisdom; to Ellen Bitterman for her thoughtful proofreading and insights; to the staff at Epigraph Publishing Service for helping bring this book to life; and to Craig St. Clair for his never-ending encouragement in seeing this project through.

ABOUT THE AUTHOR

A practitioner of trained-memory methods since his teenage years, Brent Sverdloff has helped countless students and professionals improve their powers of recall. Since 2004, he has led memory workshops at colleges, conferences, wellness retreats, and private businesses around the country. He is also the author of *How Could I Forget You! A Creative Way to Remember Names and Faces.*

His professional career also includes long stints at cultural and educational nonprofits on both coasts. Brent held archival research positions at the Getty Research Institute and Harvard Business School; marketing and communications jobs at a contemporary art museum and performing arts conservatory; and executive director posts at a theater company, literary translation center, and community relations organization, all in San Francisco. More recently, he has taught liberal arts courses at colleges in the Northeast.

www.ingramcontent.com/pod-product-compliance
Lightning Source LLC
Chambersburg PA
CBHW022007080426

42733CB00007B/505